A Handbook of
GREENHOUSE
and
CONSERVATORY
PLANTS

Anne Swithinbank

CHRISTOPHER HELM
London

© 1989 Anne Swithinbank
Line illustrations by Helen Hiles and Sharon Perks
Christopher Helm (Publishers) Ltd, Imperial House,
21–25 North Street, Bromley, Kent BR1 1SD

ISBN 0-7470-3010-3

A CIP catalogue record for this book
is available from the British Library

Typeset by Paston Press, Loddon, Norfolk
Printed and bound in Great Britain by Biddles Ltd,
Guildford and Kings Lynn

Acknowledgements

My first thanks must go to my parents, Valerie and Alf Cozens, who bought me
my first greenhouse—although I think it had as much to do with a vain hope
that it might have accommodated some of the plants that filled my bedroom as a
desire for me to acquire still more.

During my five years at Wisley I learnt a lot about glasshouse plants. Ray
Waite, the Superintendent of the Glass Department, was my long-suffering
boss and I am grateful for his help, advice and support during that time. I also
thank all the other members of staff and students with whom I worked and
shared enthusiasm for the plants.

Bernard Alfieri was responsible for some of the colour photographs I have
used. I thank him not only for allowing me to use them but for brightening up
many mornings with his presence and amusing stories during his photographic
visits. The most excellent line drawings of plants were done by Helen Hiles, an
ex-Wisley student. I am sure her familiarity with the plants was a great help in
her understanding of how they should be portrayed. Again, thanks to the staff
at Wisley for helping her find the plants she needed to draw.

Finally, I must thank my husband John for his consistent patience with a
frequently tired and preoccupied wife. Also for his invaluable advice as a fellow
horticulturalist.

Contents

Introduction

Although involved in all types of gardening, from growing vegetables to planning gardens and from growing alpines to pruning shrubs, I shall always return to greenhouse gardening (glasshouses for the professionals) as one of my favourite areas. I suppose to people who have not 'got the bug' it must seem a very strange thing to do; to grow exotic plants in a hostile climate by creating the circumstances they need under the protection of glass. However, many of the plants reward their enthusiastic grower with wonderfully exotic flowers and, often, very long flowering periods. Others of these plants might not qualify for the description of 'pretty' or even 'attractive', but are nevertheless curious enough to look as if they might just as easily have landed from another planet as grown from seed. Some are masters of camouflage taking on the appearance of boulders or pebbles. It is the strangest specimens that hold the most interest for me. If you are not very careful the plants almost seem to take on a character of their own; the acknowledgement of which can lead to concerned friends suspecting one of being more than a little eccentric.

For five years as supervisor of the glasshouses at the RHS Garden, Wisley, I had the wonderful experience of being able to pursue my hobby at work. The best time of the day was very early in the morning at 7.30 when we started work. There is nothing quite like the smell of a greenhouse at that time; a mixture of humidity with the scent of blossoms and damp earth. However small your greenhouse the magic is the same.

I am not going to talk about how to get the most out of your small greenhouse. To do that I would have to talk about growing vegetables and using the space for the propagation of hardy trees and shrubs as well. In this book I am concerned with how to grow a wide range of tender and exotic plants purely as a hobby, for the joy and satisfaction of seeing them develop and flower.

The biggest restriction placed upon the amateur grower is heat. Having installed the greenhouse and basic equipment, the costs of running and even stocking the house are minimal except for the annual heating bill. Early on it pays to work out the minimum temperature which can be maintained in winter as this will determine which plants can be grown. With this in mind I have graded all the plants in the A to Z section to indicate the minimum temperature they require.

Chapter One

Greenhouses and Equipment

Choosing and Siting

It is important to choose the right type of greenhouse to suit your needs. Before rushing out to buy, stop and consider the following points. Whether to choose wood or aluminium will be the first decision. Aluminium will let in more light during winter and is usually cheaper than wood. It is possible to obtain wood-coloured aluminium which is less glaring than the usual. One of the main advantages is that broken panes are easier to replace as they are fixed by simple clips rather than having to be puttied into wood, although modern wooden houses now have very simple fixings. Disadvantages are that aluminium causes more condensation as temperatures drop and, of course, it is far less attractive than wood. To me this is a major point as, especially in a small garden, the appearance of the greenhouse is important. Western red cedar is the best timber to choose as it contains natural oil which conditions the wood and renders it rot proof. Nevertheless it will still pay to treat it with preservative as much for aesthetic reasons as to prevent a slightly cracked looking appearance on older houses. Interior fittings are simpler to install in wood. They can easily be nailed or pinned into place without special pins and clips.

If you intend to grow tomatoes or tall-growing plants a house with glass going right down to the ground on one side will be needed. Staging is often composed of slats. During summer this can be a disadvantage as some plants dry out far too quickly whilst you are out at work. Staging composed of a shallow tray will make installation of capillary matting and automatic watering systems far easier.

Ventilation is extremely important and usually insufficient in most amateur houses. Check how much is provided, especially in the roof. Availability of extra vent units for the roof or louvres for the side provided by the same company is relevant.

Always choose the largest house you can afford because I can guarantee you will never have enough space. Economise on length instead of width if necessary. Sometimes it is possible to buy extensions from the same manufacturer. Bear this in mind when siting the house.

1

The ideal site for a greenhouse should be where it will receive plenty of light and not be overshadowed by buildings or trees. Protection from cold north-easterly winds will help prevent heat loss during winter. A north-south orientation may well admit light more evenly during the day but I prefer an east-west alignment. More light is admitted during winter and you effectively get a north- and a south-facing side so that sun- or shade-loving plants can be positioned accordingly.

Apart from the usual rectagonal shape it is possible to buy attractive many-sided houses, usually with six sides, which are often more expensive but can form a pleasing feature in the right garden. Staging and other equipment then has to be chosen to fit these houses and is best bought from the same firm. Lean-to houses which fit against, usually, a house wall are excellent for their convenience and also because electric or gas fuelled heating is easily available. Going upmarket to conservatories which are also house extensions, these will benefit from built in double glazing and shading in the form of blinds or screens. Foundations must be adequate to take the added weight of extra glazing. With such a structure it is worth considering UPVC which although expensive is so much more trouble free and long lasting in comparison with wood.

Before looking for a greenhouse or conservatory think carefully about what sort of plants are to be grown—and make a list of all the above requirements you anticipate needing. This will save a lot of trouble when you sort through catalogues or visit the local retail outlet and save an expensive mistake or regrets in the future.

Major Equipment

At the same time as budgeting for a new greenhouse it is necessary to include at least the essential items of equipment associated with day-to-day running. Heating the greenhouse in winter will be a major cost and an early decision as to the minimum winter temperature you intend to maintain is important as this will determine which plants can be grown. Each genus of plants in the A to Z chapter is coded so that it should be easy to pick out plants for each temperature range. FF frost free only; C cool (minimum of 7°C (45°F)) W warm (minimum of 13°C (55°F)) T tropical (minimum of 18°C (65°F)).

Heating

Paraffin heaters are the cheapest but in my opinion they are often inadequate when the weather turns really cold and, except for larger more expensive models, are not thermostatically controlled. Human error is also involved as they might run out of fuel at a crucial time resulting in the loss of the plant collection. The same can be said of some bottled gas heaters, although it is possible to buy those that have a gauge to show how much gas has been used.

Another reason for disliking these is that both paraffin and gas heaters give off a lot of moisture making the air more humid than is desirable in winter and increasing condensation. A small amount of ventilation must always be kept on with both of these to allow air to circulate and to allow harmful gases to escape. However, if your greenhouse is a long way from the house it may prove impossible or too expensive to run a source of electricity down to it. There is also the possibility of power failures to consider. I would always keep some sort of independent power source heater standing by in case of an emergency.

Electric heating will always be my favourite as it is relatively trouble free. This will mostly be in the form of a thermostatically controlled fan heater. Some models will allow the fan to work without heat which is most useful for keeping the air moving thus avoiding problems such as Botrytis (grey mould) during winter. In the summer it will have a cooling effect. Obviously the heater is turned on continuously during winter and should start whenever the temperature drops below the minimum you have set.

Thermometers

A maximum/minimum thermometer is necessary for you to know how low the temperature drops at night and thus how effective your heater is at the setting you have chosen. It will also tell you how warm your greenhouse has been during a hot summer's day while you were out and your plants were sizzling. A good thermometer is a good troubleshooter.

Insulation

Hand in hand with heating is good insulation during winter otherwise you are throwing money away through the roof. Bubble plastic is the most effective insulator of roof and sides. There is no problem with attaching it to a wooden house but special clips will be needed for aluminium houses. The idea is to make as complete an inner shell as possible with a 2 cm ($\frac{3}{4}$ in) gap between the insulation and the glass. Further reduction in heating can be made, especially in larger houses, by the fixing of a thermal screen. This is like a false ceiling which cuts down the volume of the greenhouse. Special material should be used which will allow air to pass through yet keep heat trapped below. The material should be fixed so that it can be pulled across at night and back in the morning to allow maximum light on to the plants.

Shading

As the intensity and height of the sun increases towards summer, shading will become necessary particularly for young seedlings and plants such as *Saintpaulia* (African Violets) and more tropical plants. Ideally, shading should be in the form of a roll which can be attached to the outside or inside of the greenhouse and let down when the sun is strong but up again when weather is cloudy, thus giving the plants more light. Ease of fixing such attachments on to the house should be discussed at purchase time. However, not only are these expensive but you have to know that you will be diligent enough to operate them at the correct time. If diligence or purse are questionable then go for the sort of shading that is applied as a wash to the glass. Most of these can be wiped off at the end of the summer. This is not as easy as it sounds and a hose pipe and broom are usually required. If plants are to be grown in the greenhouse during winter it is essential to remove the shading to admit as much light as possible. It is, in any case, a good plan to wash down the outside to get rid of dirt and moss.

Time Savers

Automatic vent openers can be set to open the vents at a preset temperature and are available for both roof vents and louvres. Providing there is a tap near the greenhouse there are a wide choice of watering systems that can be fitted. Either capillary matting or sand will be needed on the staging. A cistern and ball cock or reservoir bag feeding a constant level water tray fitted to the side of the bench often form the basis of keeping the matting moist. It is also possible to gear up pipes which allow water to flow on to the matting or even through thin 'spaghetti' tubes into individual pots. Whichever method or model is chosen I am afraid that although they sound good they are nowhere near dependable and will need constant monitoring and cleaning. One of the main problems is that algae sometimes clog up the whole system. Another is when too much water is allowed on to the matting or pots causing plants to die of overwatering.

Spraying and Misting

For easy or automatic damping down spray units consisting of tubes and nozzles can be fitted. These can be either above the plants for damping the foliage or below the staging for the floor. Misting is usually installed to help cuttings root and seeds germinate. A film of water is maintained on the leaves of cuttings which cuts down the stress caused by water loss. Seed trays which might otherwise dry out are in no danger of doing so at that critical stage when the tiny root and shoot are emerging from the seed. Both sprayers and misters can be regulated by controllers. Some are in the form of timers but mist should be controlled by an electronic leaf or by a light sensitive system. I prefer the leaf system which introduces a sensitive surface which, when it becomes dry, turns the mist on until it is wet again. Regular cleaning of the 'leaf' surface is necessary but never touch it with fingers which could be greasy.

Propagators

For a good success rate with both cuttings and seed germination the propagator is an essential piece of equipment. Ideally they should be heated with thermostatic control and have a lid of sufficient height to take most cuttings. The advantages are that regardless of how cold the greenhouse is they can provide a microclimate of precisely the temperature required for germination or rooting. This makes the most of your investment in buying seed. The only drawback could be supply of electricity. It is possible to buy soil warming cables for heated benches or home-made propagators.

Chapter Two

Cultivation

Routine

Keeping a collection of greenhouse plants in a healthy and successful way requires the same sort of attitude as caring for a small zoo of animals. I find it helpful to establish a routine otherwise I can always find something more important to do than go into the greenhouse.

The best time to do most of the checking is in the morning. The first task is to check round any equipment that you rely on and make sure it is all running. Read the temperature on the thermometer and note the maximum from the previous day and the minimum night temperature. If you have time, it is interesting to note these down for comparisons with other years, or if a plant suddenly goes into a decline this can frequently be linked to a below or above average temperature. Be sure to reset the thermometer ready for it to register the new maximum.

Be as aware of the weather as possible and set the vents and, if necessary, shading, to cope with the anticipated weather for the rest of the day. During the warmer summer months it must be realised that ventilation, shading, watering and damping down may have to be checked as many as three times spread out during the day. For enthusiasts who are out at work all day it helps to plan at an early stage for some automatic systems to cope with this. I am not saying it is impossible to do without these checks but it makes the difference between getting by and really doing well with the plants.

Cleaning

Cleaning the plants is more important than most people realise. The eggs of pests and spores of harmful fungi linger in the dead leaves and debris and hatch out to infect the plants again if they are not cleared away. Take off dead leaves and flowers, pull away any weeds from the pots and take any rubbish away from staging or floor. Sweep or rake the floor and remove the rubbish from the greenhouse. I take this opportunity to thoroughly inspect my plants as I clean

6

them up. I notice signs of attack from pests or fungal diseases, especially mildew and damping off disease on seedlings.

Whilst going through the plants I find I can really appreciate them, noticing how much growth each has put on and checking their progress. If you use the greenhouse as a holding and growing on place for plants that are being used in the house or conservatory, this is a very good time to change any sorry looking plants around. Bring the ailing specimens back so that they can be sorted out and replace them with fresh plants when the routine is completed.

When more time can be found it is often necessary to give the plant leaves a more thorough clean. If there have been problems with pests leaves tend to become covered with sticky 'honeydew' which is secreted by the insects. This gives rise to the growth of sooty mould which lives off the honeydew. While not attacking the leaf, it masks out the sunlight that the leaf needs to absorb and looks most unsightly. I have never been able to find a chemical which would kill the sooty mould and enable it to be washed off the leaf. The best, although rather laborious, method would seem to be to add a tiny drop of washing up liquid to water and gently wipe the mess off with some dampened kitchen paper. Plants that have become dusty can be washed in the same way. A good idea is to brush the dust off first with a small soft paintbrush which prevents a paste of dust and water forming. Hairy-leaved plants are cleaned effectively by brushing alone. I dislike all forms of proprietary leaf shines and cleaners as they can harm some plants, especially the new leaves. I would not risk using them on any of my collection.

Watering, Humidity and Damping Down

Having cleaned the plants up it should be part of the morning routine to check each plant for water. It is particularly important that plants are not overwatered during the winter. A combination of cold and damp makes them far more vulnerable to low temperature. If you decide that they must be watered it is best to do this in the morning so that the plant and its surroundings have a chance to dry out before temperatures drop at night. During summer when the temperatures are high try and anticipate the watering requirements of the plant for the whole day so that it is unlikely to be under the stress of needing water while you are at work or otherwise occupied. The only sure way to see whether a plant needs water is to look at the surface of the soil in the pot or border. During summer and warm weather if the soil is crumbly and no water can be squeezed between the fingers then watering is necessary. During cold weather the top 2.5 cm (1 in) or so of compost can be allowed to dry out between waterings. A plant in fairly dry soil is much more able to withstand frost than the same plant in wet soil.

Having decided that watering is necesesary make sure that the plant gets plenty of it. Dribbling a few drops into the pot will result in only the top 2.5 cm (1 in) or so becoming watered, while the roots in the bottom of the pot slowly

7

die. The biggest danger is overwatering. Very few plants can survive in soil that is continuously wet. The roots need to breathe so there must be a chance for air to get back into the spaces in the soil before they are filled with water again. Failure to do this results in the roots suffocating, dying, rotting off and no longer being able to absorb water. As a result of this the whole plant will then collapse and die, believe it or not, from lack of water. The only cure for an overwatered plant is to let it dry out again as much and as fast as possible without the plant shrivelling. New roots will then grow. The temptation is to repot the plant into fresh soil. In my experience, however, this almost always kills the plant off. Quite possibly the few remaining minute live roots are torn off in the efforts to repot.

While in the greenhouse watering this is an excellent time to check humidity, which is the amount of water vapour in the air. In the winter this will not be such a problem except in very tropical houses. However, during the summer a greenhouse can be a very arid place. You will know when the humidity is low instinctively and should damp down by splashing water all over the floor, staging and even the plants themselves (although not in full sun as this will lead to scorch). In very hot weather the watering should be checked again and the house damped down in the middle of the day and at the end. With a big collection of plants it may be worth installing electronic under-bench misting devices and capillary matting which can be kept moist by an automatic system.

If everybody is like me they will not be able to resist having a mixed collection of different types of plants from different parts of the world; obviously they will have different requirements. Cacti, succulents, *Pelargonium, Sansevieria* and bulbs, for instance, will not need to be checked more than once a day at the most for watering and humidity. However, more tropical plants are much more demanding. At the most extreme are the epiphytes. These are plants which naturally grow by attaching themselves to trees rather than the ground. They are usually found in areas of very high natural humidity and can find all they want by absorbing water and nutrients from the atmosphere or drips from the trees. Most orchids are epiphytic although they can mostly be grown in pots in a special compost. Air Plants, however, which are mostly in the genus *Tillandsia,* will not grow in any kind of compost and need a very difficult balance of humidity with good air circulation.

Feeding

Assuming that the fresh potting compost used contained a good balanced fertiliser, a newly potted plant will not need feeding for about one month. As soon as the roots begin to reach out to the sides of the new pot and the plant is taking off again it should be fed. I find it helps to designate a feeding day otherwise I would forget altogether, and while plants would probably not die without being fed, they are certainly not able to do as well as they could. The best method of feeding is to liquid feed by diluting the recommended amount of fertiliser into a can and watering it in. It is unwise to feed either a dry plant or a very wet plant, so try to manage the watering so that by feeding day the plants are exactly right to take it up.

During spring and summer while most plants are actively growing feeding should be weekly. For normal growth a well-balanced, slightly high nitrogen feed is best. Choose one which contains trace elements for better results. There are many different fertilisers on sale but they are remarkably similar. Look on the bottle or packet and there will be an analysis of the main constituents. The main three are nitrogen, phosphates and potassium shown as NPK and they will show the ratio of these to each other: 9:3:7 indicates that there is more nitrogen than anything else. Nitrogen is good for leafy growth. However, if a plant is building itself up to flower, potassium will help as it promotes flowering and fruiting.

As autumn and winter draw on change the feed to higher phosphate and potash. During colder weather lush leafy growth could be easily damaged by frost or grow drawn and long in the lower light levels. As watering is less frequent, feeding is reduced to only every three to four weeks. The only exceptions are for those plants which are actively growing at this time of year such as *Cineraria*.

There are other methods of feeding. Slow release feeds are good if you are too busy or absent minded to remember weekly. One application of granules, tablets or sticks should last at least six weeks. Foliar feed is very quick as the fertiliser is absorbed through the leaves. Not surprisingly this is best applied as a spray. Top dressing is mostly for plants which are in such a large pot that they cannot be potted on any more. Instead, the surface soil is very carefully removed, even removing the plant from its pot to do so if necessary. This old soil is replaced by a strong new mixture.

For large collections of plants it is possible to apply liquid feed without having to dilute each lot into a watering can. They are expensive, but the Cameron diluter will attach directly to a hose. A concentrated solution of fertiliser is carefully released into the stream of water which makes the operation a lot more direct and speedier.

Potting and Potting Composts

Composts

The first question concerning potting is usually 'which compost shall I use?' Dealing first with compost that can be bought ready made there are basically two types; peat-based and loam-based. Peat-based composts are very reliable, being composed of peat mixed with fine sand and fertiliser. While suitable for a wide range of plants I feel that there is often not enough drainage material in the compost to assist the passage of water through it. Sharp sand or grit, perlite or vermiculite are the additions which enable a compost to be referred to as 'well-drained'. I prefer to use these composts for tropical plants but find that for plants which I want to withstand cold temperatures in winter, a loam-based compost is favourite. This is because I like to keep these plants very dry when the temperatures are low and this is easier to do when there is loam in the soil.

There is really only one main loam-based compost on sale and that is based on the John Innes recipe. The loam that is specified for this is moderately heavy prepared by stacking turves grass side downwards for from six to twelve months and riddling the resulting wonderfully fibrous loam through a 10-mm ($\frac{3}{8}$-in) sieve before use. This loam should then be steam sterilised. Steam is passed through the soil at a temperature of nearly boiling which kills off any nasties in the loam. It must be noted that chemical changes in the soil at this stage are poisonous to plants, this effect wears off and the effects are counteracted by the additions of superphosphate in any case.

Thus it can be seen to be a fairly lengthy process. With this knowledge in mind we can be sure that most manufacturers of large quantities of John Innes are not going to go through with all of it. Topsoil is used instead of the prepared loam and sterilised in the same way. This makes the loam far less fibrous and more variable depending on where the topsoil has come from. Sand for the compost should be coarse, clean and contain particles up to 3 mm ($\frac{1}{8}$ in) in diameter. I sometimes feel that the sand used is too small or too large in particle size. I prefer Chichester grit or Cornish grit but unfortunately these are not easy to obtain in small quantities. The final main ingredient is peat, either moss or sedge; I find that a mixture of the two is excellent, moderately coarse in texture. The source of this is not a problem. These three constituents are mixed together in a ratio of seven parts of loam to three of peat and two of sand by bulk. Before mixing, John Innes base fertiliser is added. There are different strengths of compost so that John Innes (JI) No. One is half the strength of JI No. Two, which is, in turn, two-thirds of the strength of JI No. Three. Lime is also added to adjust the pH (see Appendix for recipe).

This system makes these composts useful in that small young plants can be given a weak compost, whereas large, strong-growing types such as *Fuchsia* or *Chrysanthemum* can be given the strongest.

Clearly either of these two different sorts of ready prepared composts are adequate. However, I find that I get better results by adjusting them to my own liking. I prefer a peaty fibrous compost with some loam and good sharp sand to improve drainage. This can be achieved either by mixing a home-made compost (see Appendix for recipe) or by adding extra peat and sharp sand to a John Innes compost. Five parts JI to one of peat and half of sand is good. Remember that this must be well mixed to distribute the fertiliser from the JI evenly throughout. It also pays to remember that the JI will then be diluted. Either start off with a stronger type or add more base fertiliser.

10

Potting

Potting up is the term which refers to the first time the plant is put into its own pot from a seed tray, pot full of cuttings, jam jar of water or any of the variety of propagating containers there are. Whether a seedling which has been pricked out or a rooted cutting the young roots will be fragile so great care must be taken to handle the plant carefully. Use a small pot which is just a little bigger than the new roots is required and the compost should be a JI No. One or Two or a universal or multi-purpose peat compost (see page 180 for information on John Innes composts).

Potting on is the term describing the move of a plant, that is already established in a pot, to another pot which is usually, but not always, larger. All plants will, after a time, outgrow their pots and soil. Unfortunately, the time varies not only with different plants but with the same types grown in different conditions. A plant will almost tell you when it is ready for repotting. Signs to look for are roots growing through the bottom of the pot, the pot feeling very tight about the roots, vast amounts of growth in relation to pot size and finally the leaves turning yellow and having a starved appearance. Hopefully you will have noticed before this. If a plant is in the process of being grown on to full size or to flower, potting will need to take place as soon as the roots have reached the sides of the pot. It is less easy to tell this without experience. If in doubt, up-end the pot carefully and, supporting the plant and pot surface with one hand, gently but firmly knock the rim of the pot against a steady surface so that the pot-shaped root ball will come out enabling the roots to be seen. If a plant has reached full size then avoid repotting more than necessary as you will run out of space for the ever increasing size of container.

Nevertheless the plant must still have something to live off and must be fed and top dressed. This involves removing the top few cm (in) of soil without disturbing the roots too much and replacing that soil with fresh strong compost, preferably containing a slow release fertiliser such as Vitax Q4. Sometimes it is necessary to knock the plant out of its pot to do this. The process is also known as 'shouldering off' which describes it rather well.

The best time to repot is during spring or summer so that maximum warmth and light are available to assist the root and shoot growth which should follow. However, shading may be necessary for a while directly after potting. Avoid repotting between October and February unless you have warm tropical winter temperatures. I have learnt by experience that it is not a good idea to repot and severely cut back a plant simultaneously. I prefer to cut back, wait for new shoots to develop and begin to grow and then repot.

A repotting bench is not essential but makes life a lot easier. A small portable wooden structure which can be placed on the greenhouse staging is ideal as it can be stored between use and takes up no room. It may take a bit of time to make, but speeds up the potting process no end. Load some compost on to the bench and add a selection of washed pots. My reasons for disliking potting into dirty pots are not just aesthetic; the old soil may contain pests and diseases,

11

especially root mealy bug and the old soil inside sticks to the new soil in such a way that when it is knocked out for the next potting it never comes out clean, often tearing roots which stick to the sides. Other equipment includes a watering can, knife, stakes, string and labels.

Having knocked the plant out of its old pot and decided that it definitely needs potting, gently tease some of the outside roots away from the old root ball which will point them in the direction of the new compost. Choose a new pot that is not too much bigger. There should be just enough room for the new soil to be pushed down the sides. Pot sizes are measured according to the diameter of the open top of the pot. Generally a plant from an 8-cm (3-in) pot would go to a 13-cm (5-in), a 10-cm (4-in) to a 15-cm (6-in), a 13-cm (5-in) to an 18-cm (7-in), a 15-cm (6-in) to a 20-cm (8-in) and so on. Never think that you will save time in bypassing one of these stages. A plant in a new pot is surrounded by wet soil and the air that the roots need to breathe and live has a long way to travel to get to the roots. By putting a plant in a pot too large for it you are creating conditions in which the roots are liable to suffocate in the same way as with overwatering.

Place a little compost in the bottom of the new pot and set the old root ball on this. Make sure that the surface of the old compost will be at exactly the level you want at the top of the new pot, allowing for a watering gap. Make sure the stem of the plant is central and that the plant itself is upright. This is a good opportunity to correct a leaning plant. Carefully feed in the new soil around the old and firm gently. If there is not sufficient room, use a stick to make sure that all the spaces around the old root are filled. This is vital. Finish off by tapping the new pot sharply on the bench which will give an even finish to the surface. Place the pot on the floor and water in thoroughly using a can with a rose. Subsequent watering should be careful. Wait until the surface is just beginning to dry before watering again.

Staking and Tying

This is a very important aspect of plant care. Even shrubby plants that do not climb frequently sometimes need a cane to keep the main stem straight while they are growing and to support the weight of flowers and fruits. Climbers up against a greenhouse wall benefit from wires even if they can self-cling. However, the problems start when climbing plants have to be free standing. With flimsy shoots such as *Bomarea, Gloriosa* and young *Passiflora* shoots a good method is to attach string to the pot or base of the plant and wind it around the stems. Draw it up tightly and tie to the greenhouse structure above the plant. Always have a good supply of different lengths of canes handy, and string. This should be proper green gardeners' string or raffia—preferably not a thick rope of pink nylon. Most climbers can be secured to canes. Two canes in a pot will allow the shoots to be trained in a circular fashion, even in a double circle as is often seen with *Stephanotis* and *Bougainvillea*. Three canes pulled together and tied at the top make a tripod around which shoots can be trained. Always tie the shoots in using a neat reef knot as this will not pull undone. Cut off the ends neatly. Remember that stakes and ties should eventually become invisible. For tropical climbers which produce aerial roots, moss poles are excellent. These can either be bought or made. Take a length of plastic tubing available from plumbers' shops. Wrap handfuls of moist sphagnum moss around the tube and secure it by tying round and round with fine nylon fishing line. Leave the base of the tube bare as this end will be potted into the pot along with the plant. Keep the moss as moist as possible and the aerial roots of *Monstera, Philodendron* or *Scindapsus* will grow into it. Lengths of plastic or wooden trellis work are useful either against walls, as greenhouse dividers or stuck into pots.

Pruning

I feel that pruning is something that many owners of greenhouse plants are scared to tackle. The same person who gladly prunes a *Buddleia* or *Forsythia* is wary of doing the same for an *Hibiscus* or *Datura*. With almost all shrubby or climbing greenhouse plants pruning is desirable. Not only does it keep their size in check but renews old growth and gets rid of all the pests and diseases that may have built up on the old leaves. It is occasionally necessary to prune climbers down to clean the glasshouse wall behind them. Always make a clean cut above a node (place on the stem where a leaf grows). Most shrubs and climbers are pruned quite hard to get a complete renewal of growth from near the base of the plant. However, a few plants will not shoot readily from very old wood. Cuts are thus made on newer wood within a bud or two of the joint with older wood. When a climber is being asked to cover a large space it is usual to train a network of shoots against the wall or trellis. These growths are allowed to become old and woody with annual pruning consisting of current year's shoots being cut back to within short spurs of the older wood. This is the main principle behind the pruning of grape vines but is applicable to a wide range of plants which flower on current year's growths.

Avoid potting or heavy feeding and watering at the time of pruning. Wait until the plant has started into growth before taking any action.

Chapter Three

Propagation

Propagation by Seed

This is an invaluable source of new plants for the greenhouse and a relatively cheap way of increasing the collection. Because there are few nurseries specialising in unusual greenhouse plants they are often only available as seed. Most seed ordered from reputable firms comes with precise instructions as to how it should be sown. This information is the result of much research on the part of the seed company. In order to get the best results and value from your seeds always follow the instructions as closely as you can.

Moisture is a general requirement for germination and usually has to penetrate the seed coat to start things off. Sometimes germination inhibitors need to be washed away from the seed coat to break dormancy. With large or very hard seed it is sometimes necessary either to soak in lukewarm water or graze the seed coat with a file to speed the process up. Small hard seed can be rubbed firmly between two layers of sand paper. Some people like to nick the seed coat with a knife but I feel there is more likelihood of damaging the embryo plant inside: Any damage to the seed coat should be done away from the tip or ends of the seed.

Light is usually required for germination and some seeds will not germinate without plenty of it. Small seed especially is often surface sown not only because they are too tiny to be buried but because they need all the light they can get. There are also seeds which prefer to germinate in the dark and need to be not only covered with compost but placed in a dark place or covered in some way.

Temperature is important as most seeds have an optimum temperature range at which they will germinate best. This is where it pays to have a thermostatically controlled propagator as part of your equipment. It is not just a question of keeping them as warm as possible. Some seed will not germinate if the temperature rises beyond a certain point.

With all these variables it is obvious that the more information you have concerning the preferences of the seed the best results you will get.

Compost Proprietary peat-based composts are easily available and reliable. The major problem is that they are not as free draining as I would like, in other words they lack sharp sand. The addition of this renders them suitable for a much wider range of seeds. Loam-based composts, largely represented by John Innes seed compost, are, although the original formula is good, rather variable and can be too stodgy for my liking. There is an excellent compost available from Silvaperl containing fine vermiculite from which I have had good results both for sowing and pricking out.

Method It is essential to prepare pots and pans adequately before sowing. Overfill the container with compost, scraping the compost level with the top using a thin wooden board. Make a collection of 'pressers' of various shapes and sizes so that the surface of the compost can be pressed firmly but gently down. When you are satisfied that the surface is even and free of lumps place it on a level surface and water thoroughly using a can with a fine rose. Never begin or finish watering when the can is over the container as heavy drips from the rose will make craters on the surface. If the compost is very cold allow it to warm up before sowing seeds that will need a high temperature. When sowing fine seed this elaborate preparation will pay dividends as seed will not fall down fissures in the compost.

Sow thinly and evenly on to the surface of the compost. It is often recommended that silver sand is mixed with fine seed so that if you cannot see the sand at least you can see something coming out of the packet. Personally I find great trouble with this as the seed is invariably of a different density to the sand and they always seem to separate out so that you might sow all the sand first and a great burst of seed at the end in a heap. I find it easiest to sow from the packet by very slowly and carefully tapping the packet with one finger whilst moving it over the surface, first going around the edge of the container and finishing with the middle. If seed is not to be covered with compost I press it in gently with a dry presser. Providing the compost is moist it is not necessary to water it in. Should subsequent waterings be necessary either do this with a fine mist spray or by standing the container in water. Some seed, though fine, benefits by having a delicate sieving of compost over it which is then pressed down so that it is nestling in rather than covered by compost. Larger seed can be scattered or space sown over the surface and is usually covered by its own depth of compost. Watering in can then be done using a fine rose. Sometimes, especially early in the year, algae grow on the surface of the compost before the seeds germinate. This smothers the seed and makes it far too wet. A very fine covering of vermiculite which has the useful property of letting light through is a good precaution to take if this is likely to happen.

I usually cover fine seed with plastic film before placing them in the propagator. If you are fortunate enough to have a mist unit with a heated bed even fine seed need not be covered but only quick germinating seed will take kindly to being so continuously moist. Providing seed does not mind germinating in the dark the airing cupboard is a very useful alternative to a propagator.

15

Be sure to remove seed to a light place as soon as germination takes place. Seed germinated in a propagator should either come out when germinated or if the temperature outside the case is too low at least get some ventilation on. The reason for this is that should there be any danger of damping off close warm conditions will make the situation worse. If damping off ever occurs take the precaution of watering all seed and seedlings with the appropriate fungicide. This practice should then become routine as when the disease has arrived it is likely to strike again (see page 35).

Pricking Out

Just as the first true pair of leaves begins to show beyond the cotyledons (seed leaves) is the ideal time to prick out most seedlings. Preparation of the compost in the container should be done with the same care as for sowing. Always hold the seedling by a leaf and never by the stem which could bruise it and lead to fungal attack. Seedlings of monocotyledonous plants (bulbs, *Asparagus,* grasses) can be left a little longer until two or three leaves have appeared.

a   b

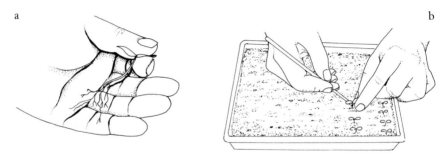

Pricking out (*a*) When handling seedlings, always hold them by their leaves as the stem is very delicate and easily bruised. (*b*) Prick seedlings into even rows, firming them without damaging their roots.

Sowing Fern Spores

Spores can be bought from seed companies or collected off your own plants. You will notice that under the fronds are rusty looking patches which are the sori which hold the spores. Keep a close eye on these and eventually they will change slightly in appearance and begin to shed spores. As soon as you notice this beginning to happen cut the frond from the fern and either place it in an envelope or between two sheets of paper, keep this in a dry place and within a few days the spores should all have been shed and will look like a collection of dust with a few larger bits and pieces. It is the dust which you need to collect and not the larger bits which are only pieces of spore case. If you cannot bear

Sowing Fern Spores. (*a*) When spores are ripe, collect a frond and keep it in a dry envelope until spores are shed. (*b*) Sow the spores carefully and thinly over the surface. (*c*) Cover pot with polythene and stand it in a saucer of water, in a warm shady place. (*d*) When the young ferns are developing small fronds, they can be pricked out. (*e*) Prick out into individual pots. (*f*) When large enough, pot on and grow on.

to remove a frond from your fern move it to a dry place away from other ferns and stand the plant on clean white paper. When the paper is covered with spores remove them to sow. It pays not to delay the sowing as fresh spores will give better results.

The best compost to use is a mixture of three parts moss peat to one of sharp sand. Fill a shallow pot with the mixture, sieving the top 2.5 cm (1 in) to give a fine surface which should be pressed down to give an even finish. It is far better if you can sterilise the whole thing which is simply done by drenching the pot and compost with boiling water applied through a watering can with a fine rose. Leave this to cool and allow excess water to drain away before sowing. The reason for this is to get rid of fungus and moss spores which might interfere with the fern spore germination. Having said this I have, when short of time, sowed spores of mixed greenhouse ferns and spores of *Dicksonia* without sterilising and have achieved good results.

It is very difficult to spread such fine spores evenly over the compost but having done so do not press them in or cover them with more compost. This is why it is important for the surface to be pre-moistened. Stand the pot in a saucer with water in it and place a polythene bag over the top. Always water from the bottom. Now a position of warmth (25°C, 77°F), humidity and shade is required. In summer just under the greenhouse staging is ideal, but in winter a propagator will be necessary. Germination can take anything between a few weeks to a year or more. The first thing to happen is that a green film looking a bit like liverworts will spread over the surface. Do not throw this away because it is the prothalli or initial growth of the fern which contains both male and female organs. Providing moisture is present fertilisation will take place enabling the spore-bearing part of the fern to develop. This is the frond part which is more easily recognisable as being a fern.

Once small fronds start to appear (or before then if things are getting a little crowded), small patches of growth can be transferred to new, sterilised if possible, compost. Tweezers are best for this job and the patches are just nestled on to the surface. When young ferns are clearly discernible they can be separated into individual pots and grown on.

Vegetative Propagation

Unless you have a good range of sophisticated equipment, including lighting and thermostatically controlled propagators, I would not recommend trying any of these methods during winter when natural light and temperatures are low. Much better returns for your time and effort will be gained by carrying out most propagation during spring and summer.

Division

Probably the simplest form of propagation is division. This is used to multiply plants which form clumps or several different crowns of growth in one pot.

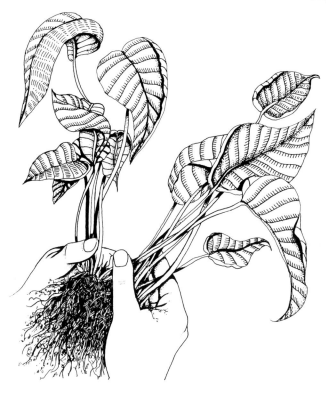

Division. When dividing a plant, gently pull crowns of growth apart to give two separate plants, making sure that both sections have healthy leaves and roots.

Usually this is done when the old plant becomes pot bound and the roots are straining at the side of the pot. Knock the old plant out by turning the pot upside down and tapping the rim sharply against a hard surface. If this is no good try whacking the rim of the pot away from the plant with a trowel handle or stout stick. Failing all else, break the pot but never pull the plant to get it out of the pot as you may be left with a handful of leaves. If the root ball is not too solid carefully prise the clump into several manageable pieces which can then be repotted. If this is impossible try putting the plant on the floor and using two forks back to back as if it were a herbaceous plant. I tried this with a vast *Aspidistra* once and it worked a treat. Having potted the new plants up water them in but be sure to allow the compost to become just dry to the touch on the surface before watering again. This is a crucial stage when overwatering can kill, especially with *Spathiphyllum, Maranta* and *Calathea*. Do not feed until a few weeks have passed and you think the roots might have grown into the new compost.

19

Offsets

Sometimes, when dividing a plant, it is impossible to pull sections apart as they seem to be joined by an underground stem. This is seen in *Sansevieria* and bromeliads. This is because the new plants are produced as offsets from the parent. All that is needed is to cut through the stem joining the plants together with secateurs or a sharp knife. Offsets are not always underground and may be produced around the top of the plant. Cacti, *Cryptanthus* and some bulbs are examples. When the offsets are a good size they can be cut or pulled off and treated as a cutting until they have grown their own roots.

Cuttings

Parts of the plant which are cut off and encouraged to grow their own roots and subsequently become new plants are cuttings and there are many different types. While rooting, it is essential for most that they do not become water-logged. A good rooting compost is equal amounts of moist moss peat and sharp sand or grit. The sharp sand can be replaced by perlite or vermiculite or can be a balance of all three. No fertiliser is necessary. It is also important in most cases to give cuttings humidity in which to root. This is to prevent them from losing too much moisture at a stage when they have no roots to compensate for it. This can be provided by a propagating case, covering of plastic or by using a mist unit. They should also be shaded from hot sun. Things are never as straightforward as they sound and as well as providing humidity, conditions should not be so close that cuttings are in danger of rotting so some provision for ventilation must also usually be made. Cuttings which dislike humidity while rooting include cacti, succulents and *Pelargoniums*.

Softwood Cuttings The majority of greenhouse plants can be propagated by softwood cuttings. These usually consist of a shoot tip and 8–10 cm (3–4 in) of stem which is all growth that has been made in the current season. It is best to take the cuttings straight from the plant but if there has to be a delay in making and inserting them they should be kept in a plastic bag away from direct light. One common mistake is to make cuttings too long. A long straggly cutting will make a long straggly plant and only very large growing plants with long internodes should make long cuttings. Nodes are swellings on the stem from which leaves and shoots arise. It is from here that roots usually develop. Internodes are the lengths of stem where nothing is going on. To make a cutting cut under a node and take off any bottom leaves that would end up under the soil. If the plant has long leaves these can be cut in half which keeps the leaf area down and thus saves moisture loss. This also makes it easier to insert five average-sized cuttings to a 9-cm (3½-in) pot. This may sound like overcrowding but in fact is the best thing to do; not only is one cutting per pot a waste of space but they will not root so well either.

With plants such as *Philodendron* and *Scindapsus* one is often presented with one long shoot armed with many nodes to make cuttings from. Not only can the tip be rooted but stem sections usually of two to three nodes. Cut above a node at the top and below at the bottom.

Hormone rooting compounds are generally a good thing as they speed up and improve rooting although there are a few plants such as *Ficus* which tend to do better without them. The powders have a limited shelf life so if you have been using the same pot for the last ten years stored in full sun on the greenhouse shelf throw it away and buy some more. I find the liquid products very good as they can be made up fresh each time they are required.

Semi Hardwood Cuttings Sometimes there is the opportunity to take a side shoot of just the right length as a cutting. It can be pulled off the parent plant in such a way that it comes away with a small 'heel' of older wood from the main stem. These and cuttings of wood from the previous year can be called semi ripe. These will apply mostly to shrubby greenhouse plants.

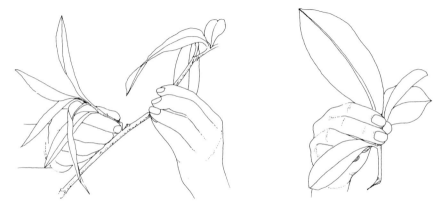

Taking a cutting with a 'heel'. If possible, it helps to take a cutting with a 'heel' of older wood. This is particularly beneficial with shrubby plants such as *Brunfelsia* and *Sparmannia*. Pull firmly down on a sideshoot of correct length for a cutting. It will come away with a small heel of the older wood, which is trimmed before dipping in hormone compound and inserting into the compost.

Hardwood Cuttings Not many greenhouse plants are propagated by means of hardwood or mature wood cuttings. Whilst giving *Bougainvillea* a prune up in February it is possible to root 10–13-cm (4–5-in) sections of mature wood, cutting below a node at the bottom and above at the top. These want to be kept at 13–15°C (55–60°F) and should root within two months.

Stem Cuttings Sections of stem with or without leaves can be used as cuttings. *Dieffenbachia* and *Dracaena* which have become straggly and only

21

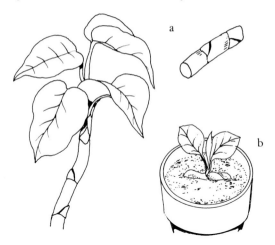

Stem cuttings (*Dieffenbachia*). (*a*) When the stem becomes leggy, cut sections long enough to include one or two nodes. (*b*) Lay these down and nestle them into some cutting compost where they will root and produce shoots.

have a few leaves at the top can be treated in this way. The best stem area is not the really woody area at the bottom or the spindly bit at the top but good average middle growth. Take a sharp knife or secateurs if you must (they can have the effect of squashing) and cut the stem into lengths of about 5 cm (2 in) each containing at least two nodes. These can then be inserted either horizontally or vertically into cutting compost. Do not forget to prune the original plant down to a small stump as it will shoot again if placed in a light position.

Stem cuttings of *Aphelandra* require only one node. Cut just above and below this, then if faint hearted take one leaf off (they grow opposite) and insert the cutting into compost so that the axil between the leaf and stem where the potential shoot will grow from is pointing upwards. The confident can slice the cutting lengthways so that each half contains one leaf and half the node. They are then treated the same, each retaining its leaf. When the container is in its final place and watered in make sure each cutting is well firmed.

Ficus can be treated similarly by cutting just above and 2.5 cm (1 in) below a node. There will only be one leaf as they are alternately arranged. Insert the cutting with the axil pointing upwards. To do this it will be necessary to roll the leaf, securing it with an elastic band, and tying it to a stake to balance it. It is necessary to keep these leaves on as there are insufficient reserves in the stem to allow the cutting to root and grow. I once managed to grow ten new plants from one 2-m (7-ft) *Ficus* 'Black Prince' using this method.

Root Cuttings There are not many greenhouse plants that can be propagated by root cuttings. However, with *Plumbago rosea* this is the best method and gives better results than ordinary shoot cuttings. Take a mature plant out of its pot and find some well developed roots. Do not expect them to be particularly fleshy. Cut off sections 2.5–5 cm (1–2 in) long and plant them horizontally 6 mm ($\frac{1}{4}$ in) below the compost. It will take up to two months before any sign of new plants is seen but they will then grow rapidly.

Toes Did you know that plants have toes? This is the name given to large fleshy roots which usually form towards the bottom of the pot and can be cut off and planted to grow new plants. *Aspidistra* and *Cordyline* are the main toe bearers. Pieces 2.5–5 cm (1–2 in) long should be cut off and, as for root cuttings, planted just under the surface of the compost. Each will often give rise to two or three new plants. It is best not to put these in a propagating case but keep them warm.

Leaf Cuttings There are quite a few plants whose leaves or parts of them can be used to generate new plants. *Begonia rex, B. masoniana* and others including the Caribbean hybrids are examples. Take a good healthy leaf from *Begonia rex* and place it upside down on a firm surface. Make cuts across all the major veins then place the leaf veins down on to moist cutting compost. If necessary weigh the cut veins down with small pebbles to make contact with the compost. Placed in a warm humid place, small plants will grow from the cut veins. Alternatively, postage stamp-sized pieces of leaf can be cut each containing a piece of main vein. These are laid down on to compost and should all produce at least one new plant. I have heard of their being inserted upright but this method did not work very well for me when I tried it. *B. masoniana* is a little more difficult and more reliable results can be had by cutting triangular-shaped leaf pieces each of which contains a section of the main part of the leaf from which all the veins radiate. These are inserted upright.

One method of *Streptocarpus* leaf cutting is to lay the leaf down and make cuts along each side of the midrib which is then thrown away. Each long piece of leaf is then inserted with the cut ends of the veins downwards. New plants should grow from most of the cut ends. Alternatively, leaves may be cut transversely so that sections 5 cm (2 in) long are made. These are inserted upright and are probably a little more reliable though less prolific than the first method.

Saintpaulia are well known for their ability to produce new plants from leaves. The roots grow from the leafstalk so whole leaves should be cut off with at least 2.5 cm (1 in) of stalk attached. They are then either inserted into compost or water. Try placing aluminium foil over a jam jar so that the leafstalk is pushed through the foil into the water while the leaf sits on top.

Peperomia caperata also roots from the leafstalk but I prefer to insert the cuttings so that the leaf is just in contact with the soil. Leaves of *P. argyreia* can be cut in half and the tip half inserted upright from which new plants will grow.

23

house, it is important not to let them dry out. This is because the flower buds develop during winter and will fall without opening if this happens. I found this out to my cost with a magnificent 5-m (15-ft) specimen of *Acacia armata* which then took another year to flower. *A. dealbata* is the scented 'Mimosa' that most are familiar with. Dense silvery-grey leaves and stems set off the bobbles of yellow flowers that appear between December and March. *A. baileyana,* the Cootamunda Wattle, is sufficiently similar to make it a waste of time growing both unless the form 'Purpurea' is chosen. *A. armata* is the Kangaroo Thorn with showier flowers but less attractive foliage. These plants respond well to pruning and can either be pruned hard back, ideally after flowering, in late spring, or trimmed to keep them within bounds.

Acalypha   T   family *Euphorbiaceae*   New Hebrides

There are two species in cultivation. *Acalypha hispida* from New Guinea is the Chenille Plant and is grown for its long tassels of red flowers which in some forms can reach 30 cm (1 ft) or more in length. It needs a minimum temperature of 18°C (65°F) to do really well, growing to a height of 2–2.5 m (6–8 ft) and flowers throughout the year when happy. Plants that become too large respond well to being cut back hard. Cuttings 8–10 cm (3–4 in) long with a heel if possible root well in spring and summer given warmth and humidity. I would favour a peat-based compost. *A. wilkesiana* and its several varieties are grown for their attractive foliage of greens, orange and copper. While preferring a tropical house it is possible to grow them at a winter minimum of 10°C (50°F). In this case they should be allowed to go dormant by reducing water and letting the leaves drop. A couple of good waterings will see them through to spring when they can be gradually given more water as light and heat increase. Prune back by a good two-thirds in spring and grow on. Unfortunately, they are prone to attack by red spider mite and constant vigilance is necessary to keep them at bay.

Achimenes   W   family *Gesneriaceae*   Mexico and South America

The popoular name for these are Hot Water Plants. As a young grower of eleven or twelve I diligently watered them with boiling water, which is not recommended. It is more likely that the name is derived from their having been grown in tropical houses heated by hot water pipes. I have known growers get good results from putting hot water on gravel beneath the plants so that it evaporated around them without contact with the roots. These are rewarding plants to grow and are usually acquired as seed or tubercles. Seed is extremely fine and needs to be surface sown on moist peaty compost. Germination should take three to four weeks at 21°C (70°F). Tubercles resemble anglers' maggots and should be planted 2.5 cm (1 in) deep and 2.5 cm (1 in) apart between February and April. Water carefully and keep at a temperature of 15°C (60°F). At lower temperatures they are slow and erratic to get going but it can be allowed to drop subsequently. If you have trouble starting them try planting them first in shallow peat. Once they have sprouted they can be transplanted to pots. After a show of exotic flowers they should be watered and fed well until they begin to die down. During winter keep them dry. The following spring take them out of their pots and be surprised at how much the original tubercles have multiplied. Repeat the process. They make excellent hanging baskets, particularly the cascade varieties. It is possible to make leaf cuttings by cutting across the base of the leaf and inserting them upright in cutting compost.

Aeschynanthus   W   family *Gesneriaceae*   Himalayas, Thailand, Malaysia

---

A group of mostly trailing plants with exotic showy flowers. The calyx is usually attractive and acts as a foil to the brightly coloured flowers. In common with other members of the family they dislike water on the leaves. Carelessness in this department results in ugly scorch marks especially if the wet leaves are exposed to direct sun. They prefer to be shaded from hot sun but must have good light particularly in winter to flower well. Fluctuations in temperature should be avoided at all costs. They will be quoted as being tropical but I believe they can withstand temperatures as low as 10°C (50°F) during winter provided it is constant. Opening vents in winter and letting in draughts of cold air will make the plant drop leaves. The only remedy would then be to cut it back quite hard and keep warm and light. Most make excellent hanging baskets which will last for ages provided they are pruned back to the edge of the basket in spring every few years and fed well during summer. The tips of shoots can be taken as cuttings. *Aeschynanthus lobbianus* is one of the most popularly grown. It trails with fleshy leaves and tubular red flowers borne in summer. My favourite, if you can find it, is *A. javanicus (A. radicans)* which has the most wonderful silky tubular calyces of dark maroon. The red flower grows out from this in a most splendid way and will last for some time.

Agapetes   W   family *Ericaceae*   Nepal to Australia

These are somewhat shallow-rooted shrubby plants which I am very fond of, even though they are wayward in growth. Most commonly grown is *Agapetes serpens* which has long stems which bear the tubular red flowers which are patterned with regular chevron-like markings and hang down from short stems in spring. If you have the space this looks impressive if allowed to trail over rocks. *A. macrantha* has larger white, yellow and red flowers which look pale pink from a distance. These grow right out of the old wood in winter. Both can be propagated by cuttings which are straightforward for *A. serpens* but can be a little more difficult for *A. macrantha*. Pruning is not advisable given that most flower from older wood. However, there is no harm in shaping up plants by removing long shoots back to within a node of older wood.

Aglaeonema   T   family *Araceae*   SE Asia

Although these exotic foliage plants will survive lower temperatures they need a minimum of 18°C (65°F) to do well. As they would naturally be a forest floor plant they like shade, warmth, humidity and peat-based compost. Excellent underplanting for tropical shrubs and epiphytic plants growing on branches. *Aglaeonema crispum* 'Silver Queen' has grey-green leaves marked with silver which reach 30 cm (1 ft) in length. This and *A. commutatum* 'Treubii', which is smaller with pale green and yellow blotches rather than silver, are the easiest to obtain and grow. *A. versicolor* is often seen but I have never managed to get it growing well. At best, it just seems to exist even under tropical conditions. It is technically possible to propagate these by stem cuttings (see page 22) but shoot tip cuttings 10 cm (4 in) long will root more easily.

Allamanda   W/T   family *Apocynaceae*   Brazil

A group of tropical shrubs and climbers, it should be possible to grow them with a winter minimum of 10°C (50°F) provided the plant is kept on the dry side and allowed to go semi dormant. *Allamanda cathartica,* the best known, is excellent as a climber trained permanently against a greenhouse wall or trellis. Beware though as this plant is going to need some headroom to grow at its best. Providing the temperatures are high (above 18°C,65°F) it will bear its 8-cm (3-in) wide golden flowers almost continuously. The best method of training it is to encourage a framework of older shoots to develop over the trellis or wires (it is not self-clinging). Younger side shoots can be spurred back to within one bud of the older wood every spring, always cutting beyond a node. New shoots will then spring from the nodes and make new flowering shoots for the coming season. Cuttings can be made from the tips of shoots that are cut off at this time. Plants will definitely benefit from feeding in summer and winter but only if the temperatures remain high and the plant is in active growth. The variety *A. c.* 'Hendersonii' is mostly grown, distinguished by a white dot where each petal curves out. The petals are arranged in the windmill pattern common to all plants in the family. The only other species commonly grown is *A.*

neriifolia which is more of a shrub than a climber. The flowers are smaller and more closed but still a good golden colour. This is more suitable if space is a problem.

Alocasia   T   family *Araceae*   Tropical Asia

These really do need tropical conditions but when warm, humid, slightly shaded and moist they grow well and make exceptionally fine foliage plants. *Alocasia* × *amazonica* has the wavy margins of its leaves and the veins picked out in white against the deep green of the rest of the leaf. *A. cuprea* is almost the reverse as most of the leaf is a metallic paler green while the vein areas are darker; undersides are purple. *A. macrorrhiza* makes a huge plant with plain green leaves which become rather unmanageable when its large rhizomes start flopping over. There is a variegated form *A. m.* 'Variegata' which has large uneven cream blotches here and there on the leaves. They all prefer to be grown in an open peaty compost and will become very stagnant in loam. Propagation is either by division or by cutting up the rhizome. Sometimes small suckers appear which can be grown on separately.

Anigozanthus   FF   family *Haemodoraceae*   Australia

The striking Kangaroo Paw, which in recent years has been available as a cut flower for flower arrangers, can be risked outdoors if it is planted in a very protected border. However, planted into a border or pot grown inside is the best place where they can form a clump and flower well. They prefer a well-drained loam-based compost, like being fed and watered well in summer but kept more on the dry side during winter as they will be far better able to withstand low temperatures. They are easy to grow from seed sown on the surface of peaty compost and given a light position at 15–18°C (60–65°F). They can also be propagated by division. Stubborn plants may be separated by using two forks back to back to form levers. *Anigozanthos manglesii* from Western Australia produces woolly red flower stems 60 cm (2 ft) high during summer with vivid green flowers that are red at the base. *A. flavidus* is 1.2 m (4 ft) high and also has greenish-yellow flowers just tinged with red. *A. rufus* is probably the most striking with deep maroon flowers and is 60 cm (2 ft) high. The flowers really do look like little kangaroo paws.

Annuals

With very little in the way of facilities it is possible to grow a wide range of annual plants in pots to give exciting and colourful displays for the greenhouse conservatory and house. Although sown at different times of the year the basic growing principle for most of them is the same.

If you have noticed enormous plants of *Schizanthus* (Poor Man's Orchid) which are usually in flower during early summer you may well have wondered how such size was obtained. In fact a lot of annuals associated normally with spring sowings can be sown in autumn to produce much larger, sometimes earlier, plants. This is true of *Agrostemma* (Corn Cockle), *Mimulus* (Monkey Flower), *Calendula*, *Verbascum* and *Linaria* (Toadflax) which are all hardy annuals but will make exceptionally good pot plants.

The method is to sow them from the end of August to October and as soon as they have germinated grow them as cold as possible without allowing them to become frosted. A cold frame is excellent for the early stages and it is usually possible to leave them out there until Christmas, provided lights are left on whenever it is likely to rain. Good ventilation is essential but during frosty nights the vents should be closed and some insulation such as hessian thrown over the lights. At the onset of long periods of very cold freezing weather they should be brought into the cool house. Always provide as much ventilation as temperatures will allow.

It is very important with these annuals that they are not allowed to become potbound in the early stages as this restricts the amount of growth they will make before they flower. Even though with most other plants you are tending to keep them if anything slightly on the potbound side during winter this should never be allowed to happen. As soon as the seedling has been pricked out and filled its space with roots it should be potted. As soon as the roots begin to find the edge of the pot it should be potted on until the final pot is reached. A compost containing loam is easier to manage during winter conditions especially when watering, which if over indulged in can kill the plants. It is essential that plants are spaced out from each other so that their leaves are not quite touching. I know it is tempting to pack as many as you can into the space but being strict with yourself will reap rewards in healthy well-grown plants.

Feed plants with a high potash feed whenever they are established in a particular pot. Avoid high nitrogen feeds as this will make them too lush at a time when they should be making compact growth which is more able to withstand the cool temperatures. The plants will come into flower during the following spring and early summer.

There are F1 forcing *Antirrhinums* which are sown in October. I like to prick them out into small pots and then pot them three to an 18 or 20 cm (7 or 8 in) pot. They will flower in May and June up to an astonishing 1.5 m (5 ft) high and, although not suitable for a small greenhouse, are invaluable for backing big displays.

Selected Danish stocks can be sown throughout the winter but remember that only the pale yellow seedlings will give double flowers. To make the difference clear you need to place the seedlings in a temperature of 4–7°C (40–45°F) for a few days immediately after germination.

Annuals sown in the spring need much the same sort of care. Hardy annuals will need to be grown cool but give warm conditions to anything described as a half hardy or greenhouse annual. *Tropaeolum peregrinum* (Canary Creeper) is a hardy annual well worth trying under glass. Grow three plants to a large plot and provide some tall canes for them to twine up. Although they will grow outside bad weather sometimes results in only an average display whereas their pretty little yellow flowers will brighten up a greenhouse or out on the patio and will give height to large displays. I sowed some half hardy *Celosia* one April and, having pricked them out into small containers, did not have time to pot them on at the critical stage when their roots began to fill the space. As a result they all came into flower as miniature plants 8 cm (3 in) high. That was a very useful lesson. I have also found that they do much better in a peat-based compost.

Browallia are sometimes described as greenhouse perennials but are much better grown as annuals as they are not worth keeping after they have flowered. Extremely easy to grow they can either be sown during spring to flower in summer or during late summer for winter and spring flowering. As they are not hardy they will need a minimum growing temperature of 13°C (55°F) to do well.

Eustoma russellianum, sometimes called *Lisianthus*, is the Prairie Gentian and is another perennial grown as an annual. This is something of a challenge to grow as it is by no means easy. Light is needed for germination but the real skill lies in correct watering throughout its growth. Endeavours will be rewarded in summer with the beautiful flowers which are bluish-purple in the species but strains of pink and white are available. Grow three plants to a pot from seedling stage to give a fine display.

Cineraria can be sown during the summer and grown on cool to flower the following winter. It is a good idea to stagger the sowings from one packet at six week intervals between April and August which will give a longer flowering period. *Calceolaria* are also sown during summer between May and July and grown cool will flower the following spring. These are described by seed firms as greenhouse biennials but the same rationale should be used as for growing the annuals especially as to coolness and good ventilation.

Anthurium   T   family *Araceae*   Tropical America

At low temperatures these plants may not die, but neither will they grow or flower well. Fluctuation in temperatures results in unattractive uneven growth giving the leaves a crumpled blotched appearance. They heartily dislike

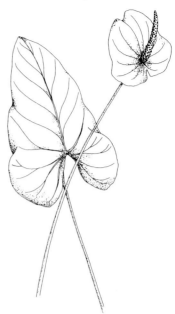

Anthurium andreanum

loam-based compost, favouring an open peaty mix with sphagnum moss and charcoal chippings. If you have a tropical house for them they will appreciate the warmth and humidity. Although they grow in pots most are naturally epiphytic and prefer to grow on 'trees' made of poles covered in sphagnum moss to which the roots can be bound with wire or nylon fishing line. Having done this they will need to be kept moist by frequent damping down, especially in summer. With this in mind it is a good idea to use a feed which is foliar as well as being taken up by the roots. Fantastic displays can be made in this way. Propagation is by division. *Anthurium andreanum* from Colombia is available with flowers in white, pinks or red. As with all Araceae the flower consists of a spathe and spadix. The spathe is waxy and almost gross in its showiness. The red ones always remind me of a baboon's backside. *A. scherzerianum* from Costa Rica is the Flamingo Flower, the spadix arising with a twist out of the top of the red spathe. *A. crystallinum* is a superb foliage species. Large, heart-shaped leaves are a deep metallic green, the veins outlined with silver. It is worth visiting tropical collections in the hope of seeing *A. longifolium,* which is uncommon. Its leaves are long and narrow, dangling down as long as 1.5 m (5 ft). The flowers are not showy in colour but the spadix is long and corkscrews in a most astonishing way. *A. wendlandii* is a great favourite of mine though not a practical choice for a small greenhouse as given the tropical temperatures it likes, it will grow huge to form a large clump 2.5 m (8 ft) round. It bears rather unshowy flowers on long stalks but the spadix of each has a wonderful bluish 'bloom' to it when young, something like the colour of a plum. Flowers are followed by bright red fruits.

45

Aphelandra W family *Acanthaceae* Tropical and subtropical America

To do well these should have tropical conditions but will survive the winter at 13°C (55°F). The most well known is *Aphelandra squarrosa* 'Louisae' the Zebra Plant from Brazil with its deep green leaves and yellow veins. *A. s.* 'Snow Queen' has bolder white veining. Both produce showy bright yellow bracts and flowers at the tips of the shoots and massed together they will give a good display. I find it pays to cut them back to within 5 cm (2 in) of the base after flowering so that they can produce a fresh cluster of shoots and avoid becoming old and woody. This is best done in spring or summer and the shoots removed will make good cutting material. Not only will the tips root but many plants can be made by stem cuttings (see page 22). *A. chamissoniana* is less showy and less common. They all prefer a peat-based compost.

Araucaria FF family *Araucariaceae* Southern hemisphere

There are really only two suitable for greenhouses and only one easily available which is *Aravcaria excelsa,* the Norfolk Island Pine. In its natural habitat it will reach 61 m (200 ft). However, these graceful trees make excellent specimens when young and do not grow fast when restricted to pots. Culture is very simple. Avoid potting on too quickly. Having arrived in its final pot size it should be top dressed annually. Feed well during summer while growing and less frequently in winter when it will be semi dormant. This will prevent its needles from going yellow. Propagation can be by seed which are large and beautiful, being some 4 cm ($1\frac{1}{2}$ in) in length and a reddish-brown colour. Germination should take place at 21°C (70°F) in the dark but as soon as this starts the temperature should be dropped to 10°C (50°F) and good light given. Should no propagating case be available the airing cupboard will do instead.

Ardisia W family *Myrsinaceae* East Indies

Ardisia crispa (A. crenata), the Coralberry, is the one mostly grown. Although even this is not very often seen in collections, it is well worth growing and frequently seen in garden centres. Growth tends to be rather slow but the foliage is attractive. They are grown not so much for their small creamy-pink flowers but for the bright red berries that follow. These remain on the plant for months so that a mature plant is rarely without them. They are not fussy plants but will drop leaves and berries if temperatures fluctuate wildly. If necessary a constant lower temperature would be preferable. Leaves sometimes go very yellow if feeding is neglected and the plant has been in the same compost for a long time.

Propagation can be by seed and none is better than that collected off one's own plants and sown fresh. It is, however, a very slow process. A good idea is to chit the seeds by placing them with a compost of three parts peat to one part grit in a plastic bag. This should be kept moist and left in a temperature of 24°C (75°F) for two months after which it can be sown normally. Keep and eye on the seed in case it should begin to germinate sooner, in which case sow it immediately. After germination it is best to lower the temperature of the seedlings to 18°C (65°F). Cuttings can be made of side shoots with heels which will root in six to eight weeks. Sometimes an old plant will become very leggy as lower leaves are lost through age. Cut back to within 5–8 cm (2–3 in) of the base in late spring, give it plenty of light, water carefully and it will sprout new shoots. If too many are produced remove unwanted ones at an early stage to allow a well-shaped plant to develop. Seed of other species, particularly *A. humilis,* is sometimes available. Germination is quicker and the plant larger, faster growing and grown more for its foliage. Shoot tips are a pleasing fresh pink. However, the berries, which are shy of developing, are dull red and then black.

Aristolochia   FF/C/W   family *Aristolochiaceae*

These wonderful plants, mostly climbers, go under the name of Dutchman's Pipe—because of their strangely shaped flowers. Not what you would call a pretty flower but definitely for those who like the unusual. If only a frost free greenhouse is available the deciduous *Aristolochia durior,* sometimes called *A. macrophylla* or *A. sipho,* from Eastern North America can be grown. It is hardy in some areas. This is the only one I have seen for sale as a plant. The others are obtained by seed which is best soaked for 48 hours in lukewarm water before sowing in the light at 24–26°C (75–80°F). Others need warmer conditions. *A. elegans* from Brazil is a good climber. The flower, 8 cm (3 in) wide, is cream blotched with maroon. *A. gigantea,* also from Brazil, has enormous 18-cm (7-in) blooms and the plant is far more vigorous, needing more space than *A. elegans.* The plants will build themselves up to flower in the summer. After flowering they are best pruned hard to keep them restricted. If *A. gigantea* is trained up a tall pillar or trellis, then encourage a main structure of older shoots to mature and cut the younger shoots back to within a few buds of these. Water very sparingly during winter when the plants are semi dormant. At this stage they can withstand lower temperatures. They are prone to attack from red spider mite so it pays to inspect them regularly.

Asclepias   C/W   family *Asclepiadaceae*

The two main species suitable for greenhouse cultivation are from different sides of the world. *Asclepias physocarpus* from South Africa enjoys cool conditions and will make a 2 m (6 ft) shrub if allowed to. Its small white flowers are attractive to butterflies but the chief attraction lies in its inflated seed pods, about 5 cm (2 in) long and covered in soft bristles. They make an unusual addition to a dried flower arrangement. It flowers and pods in late summer so any pruning is best done in the autumn. During the lower temperatures of winter water less and cease feeding. *A. curassavica* is the Blood Flower from tropical America and needs a winter minimum of 10°C (50°F) to do well. A much smaller, less shrubby plant, it has bright orange flowers through summer and autumn. There is a white form *A. c.* 'Alba'. Seed is produced in long pods and, in common with other members of the family *(Hoya, Stephanotis)*, is hairy. Seed of both plants is easy to germinate, in fact having once planted *A. curassivica* in a greenhouse border it invariably seeds itself every year.

Asparagus   FF   family *Liliaceae*   mostly Africa

An extremely versatile group of plants, *Asparagus* are excellent either grown as foliage specimens or as a foil for other plants being displayed in the greenhouse. They can all withstand low temperatures, fluctuations, being potbound and other forms of neglect. However, they are even more handsome if taken some care over. I get very annoyed when they are called 'ferns' because they are flowering plants despite their fern-like appearance and bear small white flowers often followed by berries. They very quickly become potbound and can be divided. However, their thick fleshy roots knit together so thickly this becomes difficult. I once resorted to sawing the roots of *Asparagus densiflorus* 'Sprengeri' apart but it suffered no setback despite this rough treatment. This plant from Natal has quite vicious little prickles. *A. plumosus (setaceus)* 'Nanus' is the typical 'fern' often met with in conjunction with carnation buttonholes. My favourite is another form of *A. densiflorus, A. d.* 'Myers', sometimes called *A. myersii* or *A.* 'Myers Variety'. It is strong growing and produces dense tails of growth springing from the centre of the plant. A good specimen is a splendid 1 m (3 ft) around. They can be propagated by seed. This is hard and needs to be soaked for 24 hours, prior to germination at 15–21°C (60–70°F). I keep meaning to try *A. falcatus* from Ceylon which is available from seed. It is a large climbing species, and with white bell-shaped flowers 5 cm (2 in) long sounds promising.

Aspidistra   W   family *Liliaceae*   China

Better known as a versatile houseplant, the Cast Iron Plant will also do well in a greenhouse as a display plant. However, although surviving much lower temperatures they do not really thrive under 10°C (50°F). *Aspidistra lurida* sometimes called *A. elatior* is the plain green species but *A. l.* 'Variegata' is worth acquiring for the elegant creamy stripes running down the leaf. I find that they need a lot of shade in a greenhouse, the best place when not in use being under the staging. They like to be well watered and fed while growing strongly in summer and are prone to attack by red spider mite. Do not forget to look out for their strange flowers which are borne at the soil surface and are pollinated by slugs. Propagation is by division. Sometimes a big pot full has to be tackled with two forks back to back to prise the clump apart. Otherwise, if you do not want to disturb a good pot full, it is possible to knock the plant out of its pot and search for 'toes' or thick fleshy roots around the edge. These can be cut off in 2.5–5-cm (1–2-in) lengths and just buried under the surface of compost to grow new plants.

Banksia   C   family *Proteaceae*   Australia

These handsome plants can be very difficult to grow and flower unless a few basic but vital points about them are understood. They need very good light and ventilation. They also hate phosphates in their compost or feed and are not at all that keen on nitrogen-rich feeds either. Fortunately Chempak make a fertiliser that is phosphate free which can be used. They require a very free-draining compost of equal parts of peat and grit without any added fertiliser. They are very prone to dampness in the air and overwatering at the roots, particularly in winter. However, if you can solve all their growing problems they are fine distinctive plants to grow. The magnificent flower spikes can each contain more than 1000 individual flowers. Leaves are generally long, thin, toothed and downy beneath. Seed should be surface sown at 18–21°C (65–70°F). *Banksia coccinea* has long leaves with small teeth along the edge and bright red flowers in spring looking like bottle brushes gone mad. *B. robur* from New South Wales has good foliage with velvety undersides. Flowers are yellowish-green in huge spikes.

Beaucarnea   C   family *Agavaceae*   Mexico

The Pony Tail Palm, *Beaucarnea recurvata*, now goes under the name of *Nolina recurvata*. I prefer to use the old name in case it gets muddled with the similarly named *Nolana* which is quite a different plant in the family Convol-

49

vulaceae. In the hot dry deserts of its native habitat it will reach 9 m (30 ft) in height but is unlikely to reach such dimensions in the greenhouse. It does need some room, though, as even a plant 60 cm (2 ft) high will be the same wide. While the leaves are not toothed they are very long and sharp. The attraction in the plant lies in its woody stem which is swollen at the base and the rosette of leaves that arise from it. Care is extremely simple. This plant likes a well-drained gritty compost, the surface of which should be allowed to dry right out between waterings. Propagation is by offsets when they are produced, or by seed which is best sown during February or March at 18–21°C (65–70°F). It would be quite appropriate to include one in a collection of succulents.

Begonia   W   family *Begoniaceae*

This is a large group of plants containing some 350 species and many hybrids. It is important to know which of the three main types of *Begonia* you have in order to understand its cultivation. Both fibrous and rhizomatous types, although growing adequately in a peat-based compost, will do better in a John Innes modified by the addition of extra peat and grit. They do not like a sticky, poorly drained compost. The surface of the compost should be allowed to dry out between waterings, especially in winter with the rhizomatous types. Both prefer a temperature of 15°C (60°F) but can survive well at 10°C (50°F). A combination of either being too hot or too cold with overwatering will result in the plant collapsing.

Fibrous Begonias These include the well-known *Begonia semperflorens* which are mostly grown as bedding plants and would hardly merit space in a greenhouse collection. However, there are many interesting species which are easy to grow. *B. fuchsioides* from Mexico can reach 1 m (3 ft) in height and has delicate small leaves and many pink shell-like flowers. *B. haageana* from Brazil reaches a shrubby 60 cm (2 ft) or more and has large hairy leaves which are purple on the undersides. Bunches of rose-pink flowers are produced virtually all year round. *B. metallica* from Bahia can grow to 1.2 m (4 ft) and is distinguished by the metallic sheen on the surfaces of the leaves which are reddish beneath. Flowers are white and pink during summer and autumn. *B. venosa* is a great favourite of mine. It has incredibly silvery scales which give the leaves a downy appearance and lacy stipules, which are structures that appear to bind the leaf to the stem. The flower is white. This plant from Brazil needs good light to prevent it from losing its silvery appearance and compact growth. Propagation of these is mostly by softwood shoot cuttings which root easily and can even be done in water.

Rhizomatous Begonias These are easily recognised as you can see the rhizomes, or modified stems, lying on the surface of the compost. They use these to spread the plant into a large clump. It is characteristic that if they become potbound they will go into decline because there is no space for the new growth at the tip of the rhizome to move into. Well-known examples include *B. rex* and *B. masoniana*, the Iron Cross Begonia, which are grown for their highly decorative leaves. It is said that leaving their rather insignificant flowers on will diminish the beauty of the leaves. I have not found this to be true. They do, however, produce very small, poor leaves after being in the same pot for several years. It is possible to divide the plant into several rhizomes, each with its own roots which can then be potted separately. Both these plants can be propagated by leaf cuttings (see page 23). There are many other rhizomatous species but few that are commonly available. The exception is *B. manicata,* a favourite of parks and gardens for its reliability as a winter display plant for the greenhouse. It is a tall-growing begonia worth growing for its profusely borne sprays of tiny pink flowers.

Sections of stem about 5 cm (2 in) long taken as rhizome cuttings in June will give small flowering plants by early spring and good sized display plants for the winter after that. This method of propagation is preferable for these as there is often very little material other than rhizome to choose. Some pieces may even have root attached and they are simply laid on to some cutting compost and just nestled into the soil so that they are half buried. Keep them warm and moist (not too moist in the compost or they will rot) and new roots and shoots will be made. Tip cuttings can be used provided the material is available.

Tuberous Begonias These immediately call to mind the huge hybrid bedding and show begonias which are dormant in winter and are started off in February or March by placing the tubers hollow side uppermost, half submerged in moist peat in good light and at 13°C (55°F). After three or four weeks or when some growth can be seen the tubers can be potted and grown on either for display or for bedding. For really large blooms it is necessary to remove the two smaller female flowers that appear either side of the showier male flower. The plants will die down in autumn and can be left dry in their pots until early spring. It is most important to keep them warm at 10–13°C (50–55°F) during their dormant period. In order to bulk up favourite colours the tuber can be cut into two or more portions in spring, provided each has a growing point (usually visible as little red knobbles on the tuber). Cut surfaces should be treated with a fungicidal powder and then the pieces can be brought into growth as normal.

There are two other groups of tuberous begonia. There are those that are really fibrous in practical terms but have been derived from tuberous parents and have a tuberous 'look' about them. The Lorraine begonias come into this category which are very useful winter flowerers from seed sown in spring. However, they must be grown warm in peat-based compost to do well. Their pretty shell-pink flowers are very welcome in the dark months. There are various other hybrids to be bought or grown; however they are not really worth saving from year to year and are best discarded after flowering. The other

51

group are permanent members of the collection. These are the tuberous species such as the quite commonly grown *B. sutherlandii* with its delicate leaves and pretty little orange flowers. It is distinguishable by its habit of producing small tubers in the axils of the leaves which can be used for propagation. The plant will die down in autumn and go dormant during winter when it needs to be kept dry. It is important to label these dormant plants. I have known many occasions when they were thrown away as a dead plant.

It is not difficult to germinate begonia seed although as it is so small it needs careful handling. Use peat compost lightly pressed and soaked. Surface sow, cover with cling film and germinate at 21°C (70°F) in light.

Beloperone   W   family *Acanthaceae*   Mexico

Beloperone guttata

Beloperone guttata is the only commonly available species and has become a very popular but not always easy houseplant. Given the root run of a greenhouse border and good light, however, it will make a splendid small shrub which should never be out of flower. The only disadvantage of restricting it to a pot is that after a while they do tend to become straggly and need pruning. One look at the flowers will satisfy the curiosity of anyone wondering why it should have the common name of Shrimp Plant. In fact the flower spike is a combination of shrimp-coloured bracts and tubular white flowers; an arrangement that is quite common to the family. Provided the plant is not in soggy soil or under shade it is very easy to grow in the greenhouse. Should pruning be necessary I recommend cutting the plant back by a good two-thirds to within one node of older wood all round. This should be done

52

in spring when the shoots taken off can be made into 8-cm (3-in) long cuttings. It is possible to obtain seed which should be surface sown and needs light to germinate.

Bougainvillea   C/W   family *Nyctaginaceae*   Brazil

Although originating from South America, in particular Brazil, these plants have become common wherever the climate allows them to grow. Visitors to the Mediterranean will remember their vivid blooms in hedges and twining around the balconies of houses and hotels. The exotic papery flowers of *Bougainvillea* are in fact bracts. If you look closely you can see that there are true flowers inside. They make excellent greenhouse specimens and can either be trained up a wall or trellis or pot grown and trained up canes. Their versatility extends to temperature. By keeping them very much on the dry side they can be overwintered in a frost free house, in which case they drop all their leaves, become dormant and could be pruned back to within one bud of old wood in spring, at the same time as being gradually watered to encourage growth. An added boost at this time would be to move them to a warm but bright position in the house or warmer greenhouse to promote the development of new shoots. If a warm temperature can be provided it is possible to have earlier flowers by keeping the plants growing through winter. Pruning would then be a case of cutting back only unwanted shoots after flowering in late summer. Propagation is mostly by taking 8-cm (3-in) side shoots with a heel of older wood in spring or early summer. It is possible to use hardwood taken from the early prunings of dormant cool growing specimens.

   The most commonly found species is *Bougainvillea glabra* which has mauve or pink bracts. *B. g.* 'Variegata' is very good for its creamy-white variegation. There are many hybrids with large showy bracts, the colour range including orange, rose, white and even pink and white. My favourite is *B.* 'Miss Manila', the bracts of which are a glorious warm orange to begin with but open to a very showy pink. It pays to watch out for early signs of aphid attack, which if left unchecked can lead to distorted bracts and shoots.

Bouvardia   W   family *Rubiaceae*   Mexico

Pretty little shrubs but I have never found them easy to get going. They need plenty of light, feeding and vigilance against attacks of whitefly. Once a plant is established, however, it is worth having persevered with. To keep them compact it pays to prune heavily to within 8–10 cm (3–4 in) of the base every year in February. *Bouvardia longiflora* has white scented flowers from October

53

to December. My favourite, although not scented, is *B*. 'President Cleveland' which has vibrant orange-red flowers in profusion from midsummer to November. Cuttings can be taken from shoots 8 cm (3 in) long during spring and summer. It is said that root cuttings can be taken although I have never tried this method. Seed is quite easy sown in February or March at 18–21°C (65–70°F).

Bromeliads

This is the name given to all the plants in the family Bromeliaceae. The most well known of these is probably the Pineapple. They have their origins almost totally in the New World, particularly places such as Mexico, Costa Rica, Brazil, Peru and Chile. The range in habitats is enormous as some inhabit dense steamy tropical rain forest while the *Tillandsias* or Air Plants are found high up in the rarefied air of Peruvian mountain ranges at heights of 4000 m (13,000 ft). These plants are mostly epiphytes growing on trees or rocky cliffs. There are some which are terrestrial or ground growing such as *Ananas* (Pineapple) and *Bromelia*. *Cryptanthus* or Earth Stars grow in the ground or over the stumps of trees.

Cryptanthus bivittatus

Cultivation Temperature and the amount of shade needed depends a lot on origin. Plants such as *Puya* which have rough leaves need full sun and a cool house, whereas those such as *Aechmia, Neoregelia, Billbergia* and *Guzmania* which have shiny or soft leaves need more shade and warm or tropical conditions.

Most of us will grow even the epiphytic species in pots as they demand far less attention this way. They prefer an open compost. Proprietary peat-based composts with extra coarse peat and added grit are ideal. Allow the plant to grow and become quite potbound as they tend not to need to produce an extensive root system. After flowering the plant will die but only slowly and not before it has produced one or more offsets or 'pups' as they are called amongst enthusiasts. When the older plant is unsightly the pup can be taken off. In some cases they will have their own roots but sometimes they must be treated as a large cutting.

54

While growing epiphytically in the wild, the air around is very moist and the plants whose leaves form an urn will catch drips of moisture from the leaves above. They are not used to growing in a wet compost and will resent this. Allow the compost to begin to dry out between waterings but allow water to collect on the urn. A weak foliar feed is the best method of feeding and this should be given every two weeks throughout the growing season. Damp down regularly but with a fine mist that will not soak the compost.

It is possible to encourage plants to flower by sealing them in a polythene bag, which has been inflated with air and contains an apple, for at least a week. Supposedly the ripening apple gives off ethylene gas and within a couple of months the plant will flower. I have never tried this, preferring my plants to flower naturally, but pineapple growers treat their plants with an ethylene-based product which allows them to control the fruiting. The same product is used by growers to bring pot plants into flower for the pot plant market.

Tillandsias or Air Plants need more specialist care as they will not tolerate being grown in soil. There are companies which sell plants and all manner of attractive tropical woods, shells, etc. on to which to attach them. I prefer to find my own piece of driftwood or bogwood but not just any old dead branch as these decay too quickly. The plants are stuck to their branch by means of a silicone glue similar to that which you might use for sealing a bath. This is also available with the plants. Unfortunately, the glue takes an hour or so to set so it is necessary to secure the plant with a piece of cotton while this is taking place. I shall not pretend that these plants are easy to keep. There is a delicate balance between stopping them from drying out and getting them so wet that they rot. Spray them lightly with a fine mist spray at a time of day when they will dry out quickly. Keep the atmosphere around them as humid as possible but ventilation should be good and a minimum temperature of 13°C (55°F) is ideal. During the summer the fine spray will probably have to be daily if the weather is hot and sunny. However, during winter and damp weather leave four or five days between spraying. Lower down on the branch other bromeliads such as Urn Plants can be fixed with some sphagnum moss around their roots with perhaps some Earth Stars at the very bottom. Bear in mind that these will require a more thorough watering than the Air Plants.

Favourite Bromeliads If you only have a cool house it is possible to grow *Puya alpestris* which makes rather dense rosettes of leaves and can take up a lot of space. However, it is well worth while when the spectacular flower spike is sent up some 1.2 m (4 ft) with its curious blue-green flowers with orange anthers.

Aechmea fasciata is the *Urn Plant* with its attractive silvery marked leaves and pale pink flowers. I would grow *Neoregelia carolinae* 'Tricolor' for its leaves striped with creamy-yellow and the bright pinky-red centre. As the leaves grow older they become more and more pink at the centre. *Vriesia splendens* has dark stripes across its leaves and regularly produces a long red flower spike. *Ananas comosus* 'Variegatus' is the Variegated Pineapple which

55

Billbergia nutans

is a superb plant with wide creamy toothed margins to the leaves. Flowers appear on a long stalk which are followed by pinkish fruits. *Billbergia nutans* can tolerate cool conditions in winter and has many leaves which are greyish on the underside. Greenish-blue flowers emerge from pink bracts during spring.

Brunfelsia   W   family *Solanaceae*   S America and W Indies

---

An excellent genus of plants for the greenhouse. *Brunfelsia calycina macrantha* from Chile is the most readily available and in my experience the most robust. From cuttings it quite quickly becomes a small shrub which bears its unscented purplish flowers in succession throughout the year. The flowers are deep purple as they unfold but fade almost to white by the time they die. This has given the plant its common name of Yesterday-Today-and-Tomorrow Plant. In a pot it will rarely exceed 60–90 cm (2–3 ft). However, in a border it may reach 1.5 m (5 ft). Should plants require pruning they will respond well; I have known plants flowering again six weeks after a late spring pruning. *B. americana* from the West Indies has June flowers that are white turning through cream to yellow with long slender tubes. It has earned the name Lady of the Night due to its strong fragrance. *B. undulata,* also scented and from the West Indies, is similar with creamy-white flowers in October. I have found both of these much slower growing than *B. calycina* but worth the effort for their scent. Cuttings should be taken in spring from actively growing shoots.

It is a good idea to pinch out the tips as they grow to encourage a bushy plant, although this will delay flowering. These plants are quite hungry so feed regularly or apply a slow release fertiliser.

Buddleia   FF/C   family *Loganiaceae*   Asia, America, South Africa

---

Not normally thought of as greenhouse plants there are some species that are too tender to do well outside. *Buddleia asiatica* from the East Indies has narrow leaves, the undersides being downy and white lending a silvery appearance to the whole shrub. Sweet-scented white flowers are produced very early in late winter/early spring. It can be trained up a greenhouse wall or grown as a shrub by pruning hard after flowering. This is suitable for frost free conditions. *B. madagascariensis* needs slightly warmer conditions to do well and will become rampant if not pruned hard every year after flowering. The flowers are orange-yellow in long panicles of 15 cm (6 in) or more. Take care to wear a dust mask and overall when pruning large specimens as the down on the leaves can cause problems. *B. tubiflora* from Brazil is much more compact and requires cool conditions. It makes a very good pot plant and bears vivid spikes of orange flowers.

Cacti and Succulents

I shall always have a soft spot for these often prickly characters as they were amongst the first plants I ever grew and must have been responsible for an ever growing interest in plants generally. They can take up very little space and can be left virtually to look after themselves for short periods while their owners are away on holiday. I think they are a good choice as starter plants for prospective young gardeners. Although most garden centres and plant shops sell cacti, I would advise searching out a good cactus specialist as the range, quality and prices should be hard to beat. A visit to one of these places is certainly an eye opener as I am sure there are many more different types of cacti and succulents than you ever thought existed.

Cacti

There are a lot of succulent plants mistakenly referred to as cacti. True cacti are only those plants that are in the family Cactaceae. The feature which puts them in this family is a structure called an areole which is a pad from which grow spines, flowers and branches.

Cultivation It is necessary to divide cacti into two groups according to where they grow naturally.

57

Jungle Cacti mostly grow as epiphytes which are plants that instead of growing in the ground grow up in the branches of trees or wherever their shallow roots can find a small niche. The temperatures they are used to are more constantly higher than desert cacti which might have to withstand searing heat by day yet very cool night temperatures. This means that jungle cacti will need a slightly higher winter temperature, between 10° and 13°C (50° and 55°F), to do well. Unlike desert cacti they are also in a moist atmosphere all year round and as such should not be allowed to dry out. However, they should not be overwatered as their roots are not accustomed to being surrounded by wet soil; which is also why they, like desert cacti, prefer a well-drained compost. As they would normally have the shade from tree canopies they like to be slightly shaded in the greenhouse or the leaves will go very yellow. Yellow shrivelling leaves are a common complaint of these plants and can be caused by overwatering, bright sunlight or not enough feed. Apply fortnightly liquid feeds during spring and summer.

Not surprisingly considering their habitat most jungle cacti are wayward in their growth and tend to trail or hang which makes them most suitable for hanging baskets. Plants that fall into this category include *Schlumbergera* more commonly known as the Christmas or Easter Cactus. A lot of people are confused as to why these sometimes do not flower precisely on these two occasions. In fact this group contains many hybrids which flower over a long period from the end of summer round to Easter. When yours flowers depends on which hybrid you have.

Epiphyllum (Orchid Cactus) are awkward in pots with their long sprawling succulent stems which are always unbalanced and tend to fall over. If you can grow them in a hanging basket they are more manageable. Most of the plants now grown are hybrids with flower colours of white, pink, red, yellow and orange or even mixtures of these. These hybrids tend to be hardier than the species. When established and growing well, which means plenty of food and water in summer, it is possible to prune them after flowering in early summer by cutting out most of the stems which have flowered so that new ones can grow which will flower the following year. *E. oxypetalum* from Middle and South America is sometimes seen in collections. It is a large growing plant which produces the most glorious huge white scented flowers which unfortunately open in the evening and have usually closed by morning; a good plant for insomniacs.,

Rhipsalis (Mistletoe Cactus) are so called because following their small pale pink or cream flowers borne during winter are mistletoe-sized berries which are white, pink, green or black. Succulent stems can be flattened or cylindrical. If you can keep them moist they do rather well if grown epiphytically by binding them on to a piece of dead tree with sphagnum moss around their roots and nylon line to keep them in place. Not to be confused is *Rhipsalidopsis rosea* from Brazil which is a shrubby little cactus that resembles *Rhipsalis* but tends to be more upright and bears a profusion of small pink flowers. I always find this grows better in a shallow pot or pan.

Desert Cacti I can remember when I imagined my cacti as coming from deserts full of rolling sand dunes like the Sahara. In fact a desert is classified as an area which receives less than 25 cm (10 in) of rainfall a year. Most cacti grow where there is a bit more to the soil than pure sand. The compost they like is obviously well-drained which means a lot of grit. A leading cactus nursery recommends a compost based on three parts of peat (equal amounts of moss and sedge) and one part of grit. If you wish to use a loam-based compost, extra peat and grit will have to be added to a John Innes No. One or Two.

Light is poorer in winter and most of us are forced through economics to keep the greenhouse temperature as low as we can get away with. Cacti can overwinter at a minimum temperature of 7°C (45°F) and will become dormant requiring very little water. They should not be dried out to the extent that they begin to shrivel, however, so they should be watered a few times throughout this dormant phase although the compost can be allowed to become bone dry in between. This way they do not produce any growth when the poor light would tend to make them distorted or lopsided.

During summer it is important to look after cacti well. So many people think that because they can store water in their tissues they can look after themselves. I suppose this is true in as much as they can survive a lot of neglect. However, I would rather encourage my cacti to flourish than survive which means that they should be watered and given food as regularly as any other plant. Feeding should be with a high potash fertiliser. Special cactus food is available but tomato fertiliser is an acceptable alternative. The better cacti are looked after the better they will grow and flower.

Cacti are extremely easy to propagate which should be done during spring and summer. Sections of stem can be cut or pulled off and inserted in sand to root. Cut surfaces should always be allowed to dry right out before going into the sand. Avoid the temptation to overwater the sand as this causes cuttings to rot. Some cacti produce offsets which can be pulled away from the parent plant and again persuaded to root by placing them in sand. Do not cover them or put them in a propagator as this could also cause rotting. If a favourite cactus becomes overwatered or begins to die for some reason this usually takes the form of rotting from the base upwards. Cut the healthy live part cleanly away from the base and treat this as a cutting. It is even more important in this case to allow the cut surface to dry off. Even large cacti will root in this way.

It is possible to graft one cactus on to another. This should be done for species which grow very slowly and flower poorly on their own roots. *Sulcorebutia* species fall into this category. What usually happens is that a shoot of *Sulcorebutia* will be cut off with a sharp knife or razor blade and a stock plant such as *Trichocereus (Echinopsis)* is selected which is much the same diameter as the other. This stock plant is cut across only about 2.5 cm (1 in) above soil level. An examination of each cut surface will show an inner ring of vascular tissue. It is vital that these two rings should match up and produce a good union

59

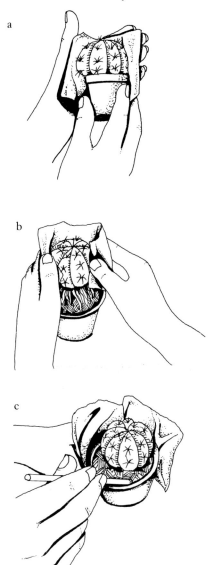

Spring is the best time to repot a desert cactus. (*a*) Use thick paper or cloth to protect your hands from the spines, while supporting the cactus. (*b*) Replace the cactus on a layer of fresh compost, either in a new pot or in the old pot which has been cleaned. Only use a larger pot if the roots are much too large for the original one. (*c*) Hold the plant at the correct position in the pot—bearing in mind that you must leave a gap at the top for watering. Trickle fresh compost in around the sides, making sure the gaps are all well filled, and firm gently. Finish off with a layer of grit on the surface.

between the two plants. Before they are placed together both stock and scion are pared around the edge of the cut surface to facilitate a better bonding together of the two inner rings. It is necessary to hold the two plants together until the graft has taken. Have the stock in a square pot which will make it possible for two elastic bands to be stretched under the pot and over the top of the graft to keep it in place. This operation is best carried out during spring or summer and kept out of direct sun until the graft has taken.

Bright red- and yellow-coloured grafts are often seen which are *Gymnocalycium* species. They are unable to exist on their own as they contain no chlorophyll with which to synthesise their own food. Personally I think that grafting cacti for the sake of it is an unnecessary gimmick. However, it is a useful technique for growing plants that would otherwise struggle. If the stock is cut low it eventually becomes difficult to see that grafting was used.

Some Favourite Desert Cacti If I had to name a few good desert cacti which were reliable flowerers the first that springs to mind is *Borzicactus aureospina*, a quite large grower with attractive golden spines and bright orange flowers produced almost continuously throughout summer. *Rebutias* are neat small growing cacti which flower as small plants and very early in the year. *Mammilaria* as a group are good flowerers tending to produce them in rings around the top of the plant. A particularly free flowering species is *M. carmenae* which is also a new species in cultivation. The flowers even appear during winter and are a delicate creamy pale yellow.

Mammilarias also have very pleasing forms such as *M. bombycina* from Mexico with its fish hook spines. *Cephalocereus senilis* is great fun and earns its name of Old Man Cactus by being covered with long silvery-grey 'hair' which makes it look like a wise old wizard. *Astrophytum* are a great favourite with very few spines and strange markings that put one in mind of a sea urchin. They like a teaspoon of ground chalk in their compost (by the pot) more to benefit from the added calcium than a higher pH. They are particularly prone

Astrophytum ornatum

to being overwatered. *Echinocactus grusonii* from Mexico is the Golden Barrel Cactus which will grow to form cacti the size of footballs at about ten years old. They are now extremely rare in the wild but are fortunately quite common in cultivation.

61

For strangely shaped cacti choose *Opuntia* species which can be moderate in size such as *O. microdasys* or large like the several species referred to as Prickly Pears. These are particularly nasty for leaving small prickles embedded in the skin of those a little careless when brushing past. *Cleistocactus straussii*, the Silver Torch, will make an impressively tall cactus quite quickly and its spines, although quite sharp, are not such a nuisance for becoming embedded in skin. There is even a climbing cactus, *Pereskia aculeata* from tropical America, which is a primitive cactus that has leaves. This climbs over a large area and flowers very well in the autumn bearing creamy-pink flowers with a pleasant characteristic smell which reminded me of wintergreen to such an extent that we gave it the unofficial common name of Rugby Player's Leg Plant.

Succulents

It is not easy to define a succulent other than by saying that they are adapted to storing moisture in order to tolerate periods of drought. However, bulbs and some tubers which could also qualify under this description are not included. Although all cacti are also succulent the term 'succulents' normally refers to plants other than cacti.

Cultivation is very similar to that of cacti particularly as to soils. The only slight difference is that they usually prefer to be a little warmer in winter and often require slightly more water than a cactus would, to prevent shrivelling. Propagation tends to be more versatile. Leaves of *Sedum, Crassula* and others will root from the base. Others such as *Kalanchoe diagremontianum,* the Mexican Hat Plant, produce small plantlets which can be detached and grown.

Some Favourite Succulents The *Aloes* are not exactly favourites but are very good plants to start with as they are extremely easy to grow. I think I was put off by looking after vast numbers of them at Kew Gardens. They were grown primarily for research in genetics as they apparently have large chromosomes. It used to be most frustrating when carefully nursed plants would have their roots cut away to be put under the microscope by the scientists. Similar to *Aloes* but I think more attractive are the *Gasterias*. Both of these are susceptible to attack by mealy bug (see page 30).

Cotyledon undulata and *C. orbiculata* both from the Cape are excellent on account of their leaves being coated with a white almost silvery farinose substance which looks like powder. One has to be extremely careful, though, not to touch or damage this exquisite finish to the leaf. These along with *Crassula* (*C. argentea* is the much grown Money Plant or Jade Tree) and *Kalanchoe* tend to grow and flower mostly in winter. *Cotyledons* virtually become dormant in summer although they must still have some water. There are some super *Kalanchoe* which make excellent conservatory plants. *K. pubescens* is a tall-growing plant with large furry leaves and bears upright

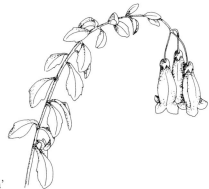

Kalanchoe manginii 'Tessa'

stalks of hanging pale orange flowers. *Kalanchoe manginii* makes an excellent hanging basket plant which can be cut back after flowering and will grow to produce the same effect the following year. Propagation is easy consisting of removing and rooting small plantlets that grow on the inflorescences as the flowers fade. Both these are winter flowerers, usually just after Christmas.

Aeonium make rather architectural specimens. *A. arboreum* 'Purpureum' originally from Morocco makes an attractive branching plant. *A. tabulaeforme* produces a domed rosette of incredible beauty and detail. This comes from the Canary Islands and ends its life by producing a long flower spike with yellow flowers.

Stapelia are great favourites. *S. variegata* from the Cape is the most commonly grown. The slightly toothed stems are green with a purple mottling. It is the flowers that are attractive, resembling a maroon tapestry. What is not attractive is their odour reminiscent of rotting meat and authentic enough to fool flies into laying their eggs in the flowers. There are other species with larger even more detailed and pungent flowers. *Caralluma* and *Huernia* are very similar and all are in the family *Asclepiadaceae* which also includes *Hoya* and *Stephanotis*—though how such sweet-smelling flowers came to be associated with these stinkers comes as some surprise. Cultivation of these is not easy as they need to be reasonably well watered to prevent shrivelling but quickly begin to rot if too much is given. A dry atmosphere during winter will help.

Lithops are small but fascinating and deserve the name Stone Plants as that is just what they resemble. In fact if they are displayed amongst similar sized stones it is often hard to pick out the real plants. They originate from South Africa and consist of just two swollen leaf structures with a small gap between from which flowers and new leaves eventually arise. Most problems with these are caused by overwatering and low light. Between September and spring no water should be given at all, a little between March and June and normal watering between June and September. Seed is easy to come by and easy to grow. They need a very gritty compost to do well.

Caesalpinia   FF/W   family *Leguminosae*   Tropics and Subtropics

These very showy plants are worth a try, especially as they are quick to germinate and grow. The bipinnate leaves are attractive in themselves and have the habit common in their family of folding the leaflets together at night giving them the appearance of having gone to sleep. *Caesalpinia gilliesii,* the Bird of Paradise Flower from Argentina, will flower while quite small, producing yellow petals and lots of showy scarlet stamens. This species is almost hardy and will grow happily in frost free conditions. *C. pulcherrima* is a prickly shrub from the tropics known as Barbados Pride. This will need warm house conditions and will bear orange-yellow petals with long red stamens hanging from them when still only 60 cm (2 ft) tall. I would say that fresh seed is idiot proof. I sowed a pot full that I collected myself. Burying the large seed just under the surface of the compost I watered them in and placed the pot with cling film over it into the airing cupboard at about 21°C (70°F). Four days later the huge seedlings had pushed the cling film off and were looking for light. Providing they are not overwatered in winter the plants are very easy to grow.

Caladium   T   family *Araceae*   Tropical S America and W Indies

Most of the plants available are hybrids of *Caladium bicolor* and are admired for their thin delicately coloured leaves marbled, splashed and veined with red, pink, white, cream and greens giving them their common name of Angel-Wings. A tropical house is needed to grow these exotic plants, providing them with the shady damp humid conditions they would have enjoyed in their natural habitat at the fringe of a Guatemalan or Brazilian rain forest. The plants grow from a tuberous rhizome which should be started into growth in March. Fill a tray with moist peat and plant the tubers so that their tips are just above the surface. They should be watered in well but subsequently very carefully while the roots are growing. When the leaves have begun to unfurl they can be lifted out gently and potted into peaty compost either singly or several together to make a good potful. Throughout the summer they should be kept warm, moist, shaded and liquid fed every week. By the autumn they will begin to look the worse for wear which is a signal to gradually reduce watering and prepare for the dormant stage. When the plants have died right back to the tuber they should be left in their pots in a warm place and kept dry but not bone dry for long periods; it is a good idea to water them occasionally. Either being too cold, too wet or too dry will result in your finding a rotten or shrivelled tuber when March comes around again. Propagation is by division at planting time.

Calathea W family *Marantaceae* South America

To get the best out of these attractive foliage plants they should really have tropical conditions. However, if this is not possible they can still be grown. If the temperature is below 15°C (60°F) in winter they will exist rather than grow and should be watered very carefully with the surface of the compost drying out between waterings. They will pick up and grow as soon as the temperature rises in summer. They are naturally forest floor plants and prefer warm moist shady conditions. If the atmosphere is too bright and dry they will become scorched and be more prone to red spider mite which is their worst enemy. At least it is possible to spot these pests easily as they stand out against the purple undersides of the leaves. *Calathea makoyana,* which grows to 60 cm (2 ft), is called the Peacock Plant because of the beautiful markings on the leaves. *C. insignis* from Brazil is the smaller Rattlesnake Plant with horizontal olive-green markings on its long wavy leaves. *C. ornata* from Colombia has thin juvenile leaves that are white or striped with white. On older plants leaves become darker and are a deep maroon beneath. *C. zebrina,* a Brazilian species, has bold stripes and appears to exist in two forms: some plants are very small whereas others reach a stately 90 cm (3 ft) without any trouble. Being used to light leaf litter in their natural state they prefer a well-drained peaty compost rather than one based on loam which tends to become very stodgy under the conditions they like. Propagation is by division, best done in summer when they are potted.

Callisia W family *Commelinaceae* Tropical America

This is a daintier relative of the *Tradescantia* or Wandering Jew. The only species that appears regularly in cultivation is *Callisia repens,* the Bolivian Jew. This little plant won fame as a star on the BBC Wogan Show. A plea was sent out for someone to put a name to the plant. Indeed, it would seem to be one of a group of plants frequently grown but rarely written about or seen in garden centres. The leaves are round and only 6 mm ($\frac{1}{4}$ in) across, being borne on stems which trail over the side of the pot branching to form a mound of growth. This makes them ideal little plants for the edge of the greenhouse staging. Short shoot cuttings are very quick to root, taking only a week if put in water. The quickest way to get a good plant is to insert the cuttings directly into an 8-cm (3-in) pot of compost and simply allow them to grow. Occasionally small white flowers may appear but they are insignificant.

Callistemon   FF   family *Myrtaceae*   Australia and Tasmania

---

In some areas these somewhat unruly shrubs can be grown outside but are never reliably hardy. However, as a plant for the frost free collection they can be rewarding, producing fluffy spikes of red, yellow, white or green flowers lending them the name of Bottle-Brush. The stamens form the main part of the flower. The showiest is probably *Callistemon citrinus,* in particular *C. c.* 'Splendens', the red 'brushes' of which are 10 cm (4 in) long. It has the added attraction of a delicious lemon scent when the leaves are crushed. *C. salignus* has yellow flowers and there is a white form *C. s.* 'Albus'. *C. pinifolius* has unusual yellow-green flowers.

The problem with these is their eventual height and straggly habit. Pruning should consist of cutting back straggly growths hard in autumn. This should never be done unnecessarily, as after a plant has flowered the shoot grows beyond the dead flower to produce the wood which will flower the following year. A really badly shaped plant could be cut right back but it may not flower for a year after this. They need good light to flower well and, in common with most Australian plants, prefer a well-drained loam-based compost. Should they require potting, this should be done in the spring. Propagation is by 8–10-cm (3–4-in), preferably heeled cuttings rooted in a temperature of 15–18°C (60–65°F). Seed should be surface sown and stood in a light place at 13–18°C (55–65°F). Plants can take four or five years to flower from seed.

Camellia   FF   family *Theaceae*   Tropical and subtropical Asia

---

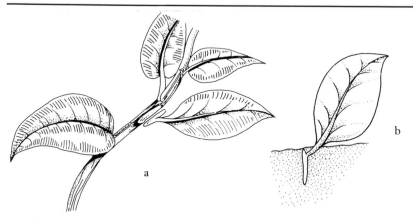

Leaf bud cutting. This method is used with *Camellia.* (*a*) Scoop a small bud, with leaf and part of stem attached, away from the parent plant. (*b*) Insert this into the compost, so that only the leaf shows on the surface. The bud that is contained within the sliver will eventually grow into a new plant, but be patient as it is a slow process.

Although mostly thought of as hardy plants there are species that are only reliable under glass and make valuable additions to a frost free collection, especially as they flower so early in the year. *Camellia reticulata* from China is one of these and exists in many showy varieties. *C. sinensis* from China and India is the Tea Plant. The only pruning necessary with these is to remove shoots which lead to an unbalanced appearance. This work is best done before the plants start into growth in spring. Plants can be propagated by ordinary 10-cm (4-in) long shoot cuttings best made in late summer. Alternatively leaf bud cuttings can be made, especially if a lot of plants are required. Propagation can also be by seed sown in spring. A lime-free well-drained mixture of equal parts of loam, peat and sharp sand is an ideal compost.

Canna   C   family *Cannaceae*   Tropical America and Asia

More closely associated with dot plants in municipal bedding displays there is no reason why these exotically flowered plants should not brighten up a greenhouse collection. The rhizomes, which need frost free conditions while dormant through the winter, should be started in February to give early flowers. Begin watering and give them a temperature of 15°C (60°F). If this is not possible then wait for temperatures to rise naturally and settle for later flowers. I prefer to let them come up in their old pots and then lift them out, divide and repot into a loam-based compost as required. Throughout the growing season they can be watered well and fed weekly until they begin to die down again in autumn. There are several species worth growing including a very showy variegated plant, *Canna variegata,* which has large yellow flowers. However, these are hard to come by. The most accessible are mainly hybrids of *C. indica* which are available in red, pink, yellow and orange. The plants can be propagated by dividing or cutting the rhizome at planting time; also by seed. The seed is large and hard, so in order to speed up the intake of water that encourages germination it should either be soaked for 24 hours or the seed coat should be filed through. Germination is at its best in temperatures of 18–26°C (65–80°F). Plants should flower in their second year. Look out for *C. irridiflora* which is a large red-flowered species from Peru. This will grow well stood in the water of a greenhouse pond. There is no need for this plant to die down if warm temperatures can be maintained during winter.

Carnivorous Plants

These are plants that live naturally in bogs which because of their stagnant nature have a very slow breakdown of organic matter. The bacteria and other microbes that usually do this are not so active because of the lack of air. This is

67

why the bodies of animals and plants are often preserved in peat bogs. Deprived, therefore, of their source of nitrogen carnivorous plants have adapted themselves to catch or trap their own usually in the form of insects. They are able to break down the insects' bodies and absorb them into the plant.

I find these plants great fun to grow. The cool greenhouse is the best place for most of them. They are best grown standing in a waterproof tray which in summer can be made most attractive. Build up the edges using logs or branches and fill the centre with peat. Plunge the pots of plants inside and finish off the surface with a layer of sphagnum moss which is not only attractive but is a good indicator that the conditions are right for the plants; if it stays alive so should they. Being used to acid conditions they will prefer soft or rain water. No fertiliser should be given as they will catch all they need. Potting should take place in spring and a compost of equal parts sharp sand and moss peat is ideal for most of them. Good ventilation especially in summer is essential. They should stand in water throughout summer but during winter allow the compost to become just a little less than soaking before putting more water in the tray. Seed sowing can be very successful with these plants. Seed compost should consist of moss peat, shredded sphagnum moss if available, a little sand but no fertiliser. Seed should be surface sown and covered only with glass or plastic and placed in a temperature of 18°C (65°F). Keep them in good but diffused light and take the cover off as soon as most seed has germinated.

Venus Fly Trap By far the most well-known and popular carnivorous plant is *Dionaea muscipula* the Venus Fly Trap, which is unfortunate as they are not the easiest to grow. As a youngster I expected this plant to be large and quite dangerous so I was slightly disappointed to discover the reality which is a small rosette-forming plant which is rarely more than 8 cm (3 in) across but does form clumps. However, leaves can become up to 13 or 15 cm (5 or 6 in) long at some times of the year and the process by which they trap insects is amazing. On the insides of the open trap are several trigger hairs. When a small fly attracted by nectar lands on the leaf it has to touch the same hair twice or several different hairs before the trap will close. This is to prevent accidental closing which would take 24 hours to open again. To begin with the trap is lightly closed so that if a tiny insect not worth the effort has been caught it can walk away. After a while the trap closes firmly on larger prey which by this time is well and truly caught. Acid and enzymes pour out of the leaf to digest the insect which is then absorbed apart from the hard parts such as exoskeleton and wings. A cool greenhouse and good light are required. Plants should not be covered with a propagating case or plastic as they dislike humidity.

Pitcher Plants In my opinion these are the easiest to grow. *Sarracenia* species and their hybrids form the bulk of these and I have found that they will overwinter easily in a frost free greenhouse provided they are not too wet. They need watching because they should not be allowed to dry out for more than a day or two either. In winter when there are no insects about the old pitchers gradually die down. Cut the dead tips down bit by bit so that the plant can continue to feed off the digested insects in the bottom of the pitcher. No new pitchers are formed at this time but the occasional leaf-like structure will grow just so that the plant can continue to photosynthesise. By spring a big bud will have formed at the centre of the plant and as the weather warms up new pitchers and strange 'space age' looking flowers appear. Doomed insects are attracted to the pitchers by nectar. Once inside they are unable to scrabble out and end up at the bottom with other insects. After they have died they will be digested and absorbed into the plant. I often cut a pitcher open at the end of the summer and am amazed at how packed with all sorts of insect remains it is. A favourite of mine is *Sarracenia psittacina* the Parrot Pitcher whose pitchers are reminiscent of lobster pots. Other genera in this group include *Darlingtonia* (Cobra Lily) and the rare *Heliamphora nutans* (Sun Pitcher). New plants are easily made by splitting up old plants in spring at potting time.

Tropical Pitcher Plants Tropical conditions are required to do justice to these exotic plants in the genus *Nepenthes* as they require heat and humidity. The pitchers work very much in the same way as for *Sarracenia* but they form at the ends of the leaves in a most curious way. The most horrid thing is when you are working amongst them and accidentally tip a pitcher over. It contains a foul smelling liquid usually with a few half decayed cockroach legs. These plants are best grown in hanging pots or baskets but must never be allowed to dry out. I used to keep them with tropical orchids and found that they benefited from a weekly application of orchid fertiliser which was also a foliar feed. Very tall straggly plants responded well to being cut hard back in spring after which they would branch nicely. The shoot could be used for cutting. The tip cutting should keep just its top leaf. Stem sections below this should be cut above a node at the top and below at the bottom with all but the top leaf stripped off. Dipping in fungicide and then the end in hormone rooting powder will prevent rotting and speed up rooting. Cuttings should be inserted into sphagnum moss and rooted in a propagating case with a bottom heat of 21–26°C (70–80°F).

Sundews These are delicate glistening plants which trap insects by attracting them to land on their sticky gland-tipped tentacles which dot the leaves. Escape is usually impossible and tentacles and leaves to some extent curl around the victim which is then digested and absorbed. Britain's native *Drosera rotundifolia* and other northern hemisphere plants die back in autumn to a resting bud from which they will grow in spring. There are fine rosette-forming species from Australasia and South Africa but I find these more difficult to keep successfully over winter. Whereas a cool house is adequate for the others I think these really need warm temperatures., *D. aliciae* is a South African in this category. A lot easier from the same area are the stem-forming types such as *D. capensis* but again a warmer temperature helps. The Australasian Pygmy Sundews really are delightful especially grown as many clumps to a pan. Also

69

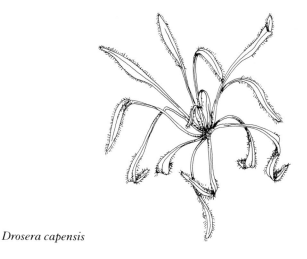

Drosera capensis

found in Australia are the fork-leafed sundews *D. binata* and its types which are large growing and correspondingly easier to keep over winter. Many sundews flower beautifully and give a fascinating display during summer. If you lose a lot of plants during winter, mostly due to a combination of damp and cold, do not despair. They are easily raised from seed.

Butterworts I was fascinated when I found my first native *Pinguicula vulgaris* in Scotland. *Pinguicula* are perhaps the least spectacular of the carnivorous plants but do have very pretty flowers. Their method of trapping insects is similar to that of the sundews. Their leaves are covered with sticky glandular hairs although they are less obvious and impressive than those of the latter. Some, including *P. vulgaris* and *P. grandiflora,* produce winter resting buds. These are easier to grow than the Mexican species which just produce smaller leaves during winter but are perhaps the showiest.

Many carnivorous plants can be propagated by leaf cuttings but the first step is to learn how to grow them properly.

Cassia   C   family *Leguminosae*

Well worth growing for their delicate, often downy foliage and bright canary yellow flowers. *Cassia alata,* the Candlestick Senna from Brazil, is most suitable for a small greenhouse as it will flower in a small pot at a height of 90 cm (3 ft). Flowers are borne in winter which is an added bonus.

C. artemisioides and *C. helmsii* are two Australian species which both excel themselves by being covered with a fine silky down. This has given the former the common name of Silver Cassia. Well worth trying is another Australian known as the Dense Cassia, *C. sturtii*. As well as being a compact 90 cm (3 ft), it bears a profusion of small fragrant flowers. My own favourites will always be *C. corymbosa,* an Argentinian species, and *C. didymobotrya* from East Africa which will bear its racemes of flowers in the first year of sowing and is often seen in Mediterranean gardens. Size need not be too much of a problem as these shrubby plants respond well to being pruned hard. It is always advisable to leave a spur of younger wood when making a cut. Propagation can be by shoot cuttings taken in late spring or by seed, which is best chipped before sowing and given a temperature of 21–24°C (70–75°F). I would favour a loam-based compost if temperatures are going to be low in winter as the compost will have to be kept on the dry side accordingly. There might be other benefits to growing these plants as they are the source of senna pods and are also gifted with many medicinal claims made for the seeds, pods, flowers and bark.

Ceropegia   C/W   family *Asclepiadaceae*

Ceropegia woodii

At first sight it is hard to believe that these plants are in the same family as *Hoya* and *Stephanotis*. Most usually grown is *Ceropegia woodii*, the Rosary Plant from Natal. The plant forms tubers from which arise the trailing stems studded with small succulent heart-shaped leaves, each traced with its own

71

pattern. The flowers are freely produced and although not showy are curious enough to be interesting. The only other species I have grown is *C. stapeliifor-mis* from the Cape so called because its stem and leaf structure is similar to *Stapelia,* another succulent genus in the same family. This grows on a larger scale to *C. woodii* and could even be called ugly were it not for its 5-cm (2-in) long purple and white flowers which are like little coronets. *C. woodii* can tolerate and even do well in cool house conditions. In fact the cooler it is grown the more compact and tuberous it becomes. Plenty of light is needed and a well-drained loamy soil kept very much on the dry side during winter. Propagation is simple, either by normal shoot cuttings 5–8 cm (2–3 in) long made by cutting below a node at the base and above one at the top, or by detaching tubers from the main part of the plant. *C. stapeliiformis* seemed to prefer warm conditions to flower well. Cuttings are easily made by detaching stem sections. Both these species can be raised easily from seed.

Cestrum   FF/C/W   family *Solanaceae*

Cestrum purpureum (C. elegans)

The plant for the frost free house is *Cestrum* 'Newellii' which is thought to be a hybrid of unknown parentage. The tubular flowers are bright red and produced during summer and autumn. The only drawback is that it grows fast and needs some space to do well; probably best trained against a wall or trellis. However, it is redeemed by responding well to being pruned very hard back to retain its shape and vigour. This is best done by reducing the growth after flowering, allowing the plant to become semi dormant during winter and pruning hard in early March or just before growth resumes. I find that *C. aurantiacum* from Guatemala does better in the cool house although it will live in frost free conditions. It has lovely golden-yellow flowers from June to September but rather disarmingly sheds leaves, until one realises that it is supposed to be 'sub-evergreen'. *C. purpureum (C. elegans)* from Mexico prefers it a little warmer and produces an attractive display from May to autumn of reddish-purple flowers with berries the same colour, all on the plant at the same time. These two species also grow tall if left. My favourite method of dealing with this is to train main shoots into the desired shape or size and thereafter prune back the side shoots to within a bud of these older growths. Propagation is straightforward from cuttings. Seed may also be sown. Be ever watchful for whitefly.

Chlorophytum   W   family *Liliaceae*

The ubiquitous Spider Plant barely needs an introduction. It really only merits greenhouse space as a filler plant to set off more choice plants in a display. There are, however, three species commonly cultivated: *Chlorophytum elatum* 'Variegatum' (sometimes called *C. capense* 'Variegatum') is the most common; *C. comosum* 'Variegatum' has a more distinct green band around the edge of the leaf, both of these are from South Africa; *C. laxum* 'Variegatum' from Ghana and northern Nigeria is more distinguishable, being smaller, with stiffer, narrower leaves than the others. For use in the greenhouse they should be raised in batches either by detaching similarly sized plantlets and rooting them in a box before potting up or by splitting mature plants. They are most useful in a 10 or 13 cm (4 or 5 in) pot and although they become potbound, with feeding they will be able to give good value for up to three years. I would favour a loam-based compost for these.

Chorizema   C   family *Leguminosae*   Australia

I always thought I should hate a plant with orange and pink flowers until I first saw *Chorizema ilicifolium* growing in the Australian House at Kew Gardens. It is also one of those plants whose name is easy to remember because of its descriptive quality; the leaves really are like small holly *(Ilex)* leaves. Not an easy plant to find but a most rewarding one to grow, it will begin to produce its bright pea-like flowers even as a rooted cutting and will continue from March to October. It is better not to prune if you have the space, allowing them to grow to a bush of 1.2 m (4 ft). Pruning lightly after flowering will enable plants to be restricted to a system of canes in a pot. Compost should be of equal parts loam, peat and grit to give good drainage. Cuttings should be taken in March and seed can also be sown. I have only ever seen one other species offered as seed—*C. dicksonii,* which is a similar but slightly smaller shrub.

Chrysanthemum   C   family *Compositae*

Chrysanthemum frutescens is sometimes called Marguerite although I am sure I have heard the same name mistakenly applied to the hardy herbaceous perennial *C. maximum.* These very attractive shrubby plants from the Canary Isles have white daisy-like flowers and rather decorative foliage. Hybrids give larger flowers and range of flower colour such as *C. f.* 'Jamaica Primrose' which has yellow flowers and *C. f.* 'Vancouver' which is pink. Cuttings can be taken spring, summer and autumn. Plants are easy to keep. Shoots can be pinched out to encourage bushy growth or they can be trained into standards using the same procedure as for standard *Fuchsias* (see page 107). They can be stood or planted outside the greenhouse during the warmer months but will not tolerate frost.

The plants most people think of when chrysanthemum is mentioned are an extremely variable group of hybrids catering for a wide range of preferences and uses. The routine for most of the pot chrysanths is the same. Cuttings are taken during winter or very early in the year. They are grown on with much attention to potting on at the right time into a rich John Innes loam compost and fed well as soon as they are established in their pots, initially with a high nitrogen feed and, as they build up to flower, twice weekly with a high potash feed. As soon as there is no danger of frost plants can be stood outside in a good sunny position for the summer with some support against strong winds. Before frosts and gales start in autumn bring the plants inside and give them very cool airy conditions until they flower. Unfortunately, they do take up a lot of space which makes it difficult for a small greenhouse owner to grow many. After flowering the plants should be cut hard back to within short stalks of the roots. Plants are taken from their pots, as much soil as possible knocked away and the root bundled into deep seed trays with compost packed around them. They are kept very much on the dry side and cool like this until a few weeks before cuttings are needed when they can be warmed up a little and watered to produce shoots.

The type of plant grown will vary depending on what they are to be used for. The huge exhibition blooms the size of footballs such as *C.* 'Charles Shoesmith' are arrived at by much disbudding and removal of sideshoots so that only one stem per plant develops and only the main central bud is allowed to grow. Spray chrysanths must be the most popular for everyday cut flower uses.

Plants are stopped once or twice to promote several stems on which the flowers can grow. Cascade chrysanths are only really for those with much space and time because to make good showy display plants out of them, huge fans of cascading shoots are trained involving much work in the way of stopping so that the small pretty flowers are produced over as much of the plant as possible. The best pot display plants for a smaller greenhouse must be the charms. These grow naturally into a small round plant which is an amazing ball of small flowers when in full bloom. Large specimens of these can be had by the usual cuttings in winter method. However, smaller more manageable plants can be grown by sowing seed early in the spring. There are of course many more different types of chrysanthemums and they are great fun to grow and experiment with. All are short day plants, needing a minimum of $9\frac{1}{2}$–10 hours of darkness every night to initiate flower buds. Of course the amount of light they receive can be artificially controlled. Personally I dislike the concept of making them flower all year round as the commercial growers do. For me the sight and smell of chrysanthemums are part of the autumn scene. Plants bought out of season in flower are often very small as they have been made to initiate buds at this stage in their growth. If you propagate from them and grow on naturally they will inevitably grow into taller plants.

Cissus   C/T   family *Vitaceae*

There are two popularly grown species which are both climbers. *Cissus antarctica* is the Kangaroo Vine from New South Wales in Australia and will do as well in the house as in the greenhouse. It does best in warm conditions but will survive cool conditions well. Extremely easy to grow, the only thing it dislikes is dry air. If grown close to a heater it might develop unsightly brown tips to the leaves. Growing *C. discolor* from Java and Cambodia is a challenge in comparison. It is much more attractive than its tougher relative, having brightly coloured leaves. However, it needs humid tropical conditions to do well. A light peat-based compost is much preferred and care will have to be taken not to overwater the plant, particularly if it is being asked to tolerate lower temperatures than it likes. Propagation is usually by cuttings but it is possible to obtain seed. Occasionally seed of other species not usually grown is offered for the adventurous to try.

Citrus   C/W   family *Rutaceae*

These are great fun to grow because of the possibility of their bearing fruit as well as scented flowers and the lovely citrus smell from their glossy leaves and bark. Most *Citrus* can virtually tolerate frost free conditions but will not do very well and are unlikely to bear fruit. A temperature of 10°C (50°F) in winter is preferable. Fluctuations in temperature should be avoided. The biggest problem is their liability to be attacked by mealy bug or scale insects. Either will secrete sticky honeydew which falls on to the leaf surfaces which then become covered with sooty mould growing on the honeydew (see page 35). Having controlled the pests, the only way to be rid of the mould is to wipe it away. With large plants when this is not feasible I usually resort to pruning the plant back hard to get rid of most of the foliage. Fortunately *Citrus* respond well to this hard pruning. Do not be afraid to cut back to quite old wood, cutting always above a node. Within a short time fresh green shoots will appear in such a profusion that it is often wise to thin them out in order to get a well-balanced plant. It will probably take at least one year for flowers to appear. *Citrus* are heavy feeders and will quickly become yellow-leaved and sorry looking if this is neglected.

Citrus limon, the lemon, flowers in spring. As the fruits take about a year to form and ripen they can be ready for Shrove Tuesday. *C. mitis* is the Calamondin orange from the Philippines. It is a small compact shrubby plant which is excellent for pots, flowering and producing its small fruits all year round. *C. sinensis,* of Chinese origin is the sweet Orange of commerce but makes a rather large plant. Propagation can be by sowing the pips. I plant mine just under the surface of the compost and place them in a temperature of 21°C (70°F). Germination should take place within two weeks but can take up to one month. Interestingly there are often three seedlings from one pip. Two arise from embryonic tissue in the mother plant and will be identical to it, whereas one will be the true hybrid and is an unknown quantity. Cuttings of 8–10-cm (3–4-in) long semi ripe wood should be taken during the summer. Lemon and Citron *(C. medica)* are relatively easy to root in comparison to Grapefruit *(Citrus paradisi)* and Orange. For the adventurous it is possible to bud any *Citrus,* usually on to one year old seedling stocks of a close relative, *Poncirus trifoliata.* This should take place in August. Grafting is also possible. Budded plants usually fruit earlier.

Clerodendrum   T   family *Verbenaceae*

The most commonly grown is the very attractive *Clerodendrum thomsonae,* the Bleeding Heart Vine from tropical West Africa. Petals are bright crimson, protruding from a creamy-white calyx providing a most effective contrast. Although this plant prefers tropical conditions I have found that it will overwinter at lower temperatures in a dormant state. In the autumn plants should be pruned back to within a few buds of older growth. Water sparingly until the spring when it will produce new shoots that will quickly look for a climbing frame. However, to appreciate the full glory of the plant it should be given its head and allowed to climb as high as it likes in a tropical atmosphere, where, providing it has sufficient light, it will flower spectacularly. The same can be said for *C. splendens,* the flowers of which are vivid scarlet. If this requires pruning, do so as drastically as you like after flowering and it will grow back in leaps and bounds. There is a hybrid between these two species, *C. speciosum,* but I do not consider it as a rival to either of its parents. *C.* × *speciosissimum* from Java is an attractive shrubby species worth growing if you can find a source of seed. Large terminal panicles of scarlet flowers are produced in the autumn and winter. *C. fragrans pleniflorum* is another shrubby species from China and Japan which can do well at lower temperatures. It has white double flowers suffused with pink and heavily scented. Both these grow to 1.2 m (4 ft). Seed sown when ripe or in the spring should yield flowering plants by the following season. Cuttings of side shoots 8–10 cm (3–4 in) long should root easily at 21°C (70°F) and it is worth looking around the base of plants for detachable suckers. Have a go at taking root cuttings although I cannot vouch for this myself.

Clianthus   FF/C   family *Leguminosae*   Australasia and Far East

---

Clianthus puniceus 'Albus'

Clianthus puniceus from New Zealand makes a very useful shrub for the frost free house. The only two drawbacks are that red spider mite are partial to it and it needs a wall or trellis to lean against. The strangely shaped red flowers produced in spring and summer have earned it the names Lobster Claw and Parrot's Bill. There is a white-flowered form, *C. p.* 'Albus'. Provided the mites are kept at bay it is an easy plant to grow and propagate by seed or cuttings. The same cannot be said of *C. formosus,* sometimes known as *C. dampieri.* This is the Glory Pea of Australia and it really is difficult to grow. They will germinate quite well from seed but quickly go into a decline. I did see a batch brought on to flower at 30 cm (1 ft) high but they very shortly died. The solution is to graft them on to a close relative, *Colutea arborescens* or Bladder Senna, when both are at seedling stage. Good seed firms will sell both seed as a 'kit' with full instructions. This species will also need warmer conditions.

Clivia   W   family *Amaryllidaceae*   South Africa

The bright orange-coloured flowers of *Clivia miniata* will brighten any greenhouse in the spring. There are also some lovely hybrids with yellow or creamy-orange flowers, and even *C. m.* 'Striata' which has variegated leaves. It is best to allow these plants to form undisturbed clumps or potfuls for as long as possible to get the best flowers. Should they have to be divided after flowering it may take one season or more before they will flower again. If seed is sown you will have to wait about eight years for flowers. This is worth doing, however, as they are very expensive to buy. Unlike some of their relatives they are evergreen and only need a period of two months in winter at lower temperatures and drier conditions as a rest period. At other times they should be watered freely and fed every fortnight. *C. nobilis* is often seen. It has smaller green-tipped flowers but still makes a handsome plant.

Cobaea   C   family *Polemoniaceae*   Central and S America

If you want to cover an area quickly then *Cobaea scandens* is your plant. More often grown outside as an annual it will make a rampant perennial indoors. Climbing by means of tendrils it produces strange purple cup and saucer flowers in late summer. When it has finished it can be cut back hard to remove almost all the growth which becomes tatty by winter. Not only will it sprout again in spring but you will probably find it has seeded itself around. It will do better planted out in a border but can be confined to a pot. Seed sown early in the year must be fresh to germinate well.

Codiaeum   T   family *Euphorbiaceae*   Malaya and Pacific Isles

---

These attractive foliage plants with their brightly coloured leaves, earning them the name Joseph's Coat or Croton, really need tropical conditions to do well. Lower temperatures result in growth stopping, whereas fluctuations will cause leaves to drop. However, given the conditions they like they will mostly make 1.5-m (5-ft) specimens in pots before becoming leggy. There are many named varieties to choose from derived from the main species *Codiaeum variegatum pictum* but if you get them mixed up it is almost impossible to sort them out. It is common to see several completely different coloured leaves on each plant according to maturity and light. If they become leggy, cut the stems back hard and given good light they will shoot again in spring. This is a good time to root cuttings 8–10 cm (3–4 in) long. When doing this it is advisable to reduce the length of the leaves to make them more manageable. Mealy bug are the only pest liable to cause serious problems but are easily controlled if spotted soon enough.

Coffea   W   family *Rubiaceae*   Ethiopia

Coffea arabica is worth growing for its attractive glossy foliage as well as for its white fragrant star-shaped flowers borne along the stems in summer. These are followed by red fruits, each of which contain two seeds which are the coffee beans which roasted, ground and brewed end up in our coffee cups. Planted in a border this plant will reach 2 or 2.5 m (7 or 8 ft) but pot grown will stay at 1.2 m (4 ft). For those short of room it is useful to know about *C. a.* 'Nana', which is the dwarf form, flowering and fruiting while only 45 cm (1½ ft) tall. Watch out for attacks of scale insect or mealy bug, the honeydew from which will encourage sooty mould to form on the leaf surfaces. Any pruning should be done in spring when cuttings can also be tried although they are not easy. Soak seed for 48 hours before sowing in the light at 21–26°C (70–80°F) in March.

Coleus   W   family *Labiatae*   Old World Tropics

Most of the plants grown are varieties of *Coleus blumei* from Java. Good strong named varieties are available which must be propagated by cuttings. These are best taken in summer and root very quickly. The resulting plants grown on through the winter will make good sized plants the following year. Alternatively, there are some very good seed mixtures available. Having grown these you can select out your favourite colours and propagate them on by cuttings. Whichever method is being used it is important to pinch out the tips constantly, starting with small plants at 8 cm (3 in) high. This will cause branching and maintain a good shape as well as discouraging flower production. Flowers are mostly unattractive and quality of foliage is reduced if they develop. It is possible to train standard or fan *Coleus* if you have the heat to keep them growing throughout the winter and a good strong variety such as Pineapple Beauty. *C. b. verschaffeltii,* which has purplish-red leaves can be allowed to

79

produce flowers as they are a good deep blue and contrast well with the foliage. Of the species I would only bother to grow *C. thyrsoideus* from Central Africa which has quite succulent strong-smelling hairy leaves and large bright blue flowers in winter.

Columnea   W   family *Gesneriaceae*   Tropical America

Columnea × banksii

These make splendid hanging basket plants. Despite liking warm temperatures they can withstand and even flower better after cooler winter conditions. Most grow very long trailing stems. If plants become bare of leaves at the top they can be cut hard back to within a few centimetres of the base usually towards the end of the summer or after flowering. This will give them time to grow back again before flowering. In their native rain forests they would be semi epiphytic, growing in niches in the trees. It is not hard to imagine that they dislike wet stodgy composts so allow the soil in the basket to dry out slightly between waterings especially if being kept cool in winter. Never squirt them with water as they are all prone to water scorch on the leaves.

Most commonly grown is *Columnea × banksii* which produces stems up to 1.2 m (4 ft) long, very slightly hairy leaves and orange-red tubular flowers early in the year and usually again later. *C. microphylla* is attractive, especially *C. m.* 'Tricolor' as its small hairy leaves are prettily variegated and look especially nice with the orange-red flowers. My favourite is *C. gloriosa* 'Purpurea' from Costa Rica. The flame-coloured large flowers look super in late winter against the hairy purple foliage. There are several hybrids, the most unusual of which is *C.* 'Alpha' with yellow flowers. Cuttings 8 cm (3 in) long root well and are best pinched out to encourage a small branched plant. Once cuttings have filled small pots they can be planted six to a basket in peat-based compost and will soon begin to trail over the edge. Seed should be surface sown in a light place at 21–24°C (70–75°F).

Cordyline   C/T   family *Liliaceae*

Dealing first with the cool growing species, they are *Cordyline australis,* the Cabbage Palm which grows outside in Cornwall, and the similar *C. indivisa* which has slightly longer and wider leaves. They make large plants and, unless you have a huge greenhouse, it is unlikely that they would merit the space unless being overwintered for use outside during the summer in tubs. Purple- and variegated-leaved forms of *C. australis* are available. *C. terminalis,* which has been called *Dracaena terminalis,* is on the other hand a lover of tropical conditions. They will do little other than exist under lower temperatures. This is the Ti Plant of the Polynesians, who believe that it is lucky to have one growing about the house. They also come in handy for making hula hula skirts. The Maoris used to grow it for its edible roots from which they also used to distil a wickedly intoxicating liquor. Our use of it as a houseplant is comparatively tame. *C. terminalis* has reddish-green leaves but there are several forms with different leaf colours to choose from.

Old plants can be cut back and will make several shoots resulting in a very bushy plant. New shoots can be detached and used as cuttings. Sometimes plants are available in 'log' form; these are stem sections which should be put into water to root before being potted up. The easiest method of propagation is to tap a well-rooted plant out of its pot and look for toes or fleshy roots at the bottom. Cut these off and bury them just under the surface of some compost. In temperatures of 21°C (70°F) they will soon grow into new plants. Seed can be sown; mixed varieties being exciting as you never know what will turn up. Soak the seed for just ten minutes in hand hot water before sowing at 24°C (75°F).

Coronilla   FF/C   family *Leguminosae*   Europe

Coronilla glauca is worth growing for its bright yellow pea-like flowers and attractive evergreen foliage. Flowers are borne in late spring and have a mouthwatering fruity smell, during the day only, which is reminiscent of peaches and pineapple. As this shrub is almost hardy it makes an excellent plant for the frost free house. Cuttings should be taken in late summer or seed sown on the surface of peaty compost at 18–21°C (65–70°F) in spring. *C. g. pygmaea* is a smaller more compact version for those having to economise on space.

Correa   C   family *Rutaceae*   Australia and Tasmania

Correa × harisii

I have always found these small shrubs very useful as many of them flower during autumn and winter. While not being spectacular they are usually compact and floriferous, the bell-shaped flowers appearing all over the plants. I grow them in loam-based compost and find that, provided they are not overwatered when the temperatures are low, they are trouble free and reliable. *Correa × harisii* is a red-flowered hybrid and flowers in winter as does *C. pulchella* which is pink. *C. albus* with white flowers and *C. backhousiana* with beautiful creamy-coloured bells flower in spring or early summer. If their growth becomes leggy in pots they respond well to being pruned back by two-thirds after flowering.

Crinum   C/W/T   family *Amaryllidaceae*

These evergreen bulbous plants with showy often scented flowers are easy to grow. Some, such as *Crinum × powellii,* can grow outside but still need a sheltered south border. Do not forget that if your greenhouse is heated there is

82

a valuable asset in the borders that run alongside it. They will receive a good deal of frost protection from the heat inside. Such borders are ideal for trying tender subjects. *C. asiaticum* and *C. makowani* from Natal are more tender and are better inside a cool or warm house. Others such as *C. pacificum* need tropical conditions to do well. As plants are naturally found by water they can tolerate moist conditions when being grown warm. It is wise to give an occasional drier rest after flowering. Seed is simple to raise provided it is fresh. It should be sown in 8- or 10-cm (3- or 4-in) pots as the roots will be long. A temperature of 15°C (60°F) seemed ideal when I germinated some seed which had been brought back from British Honduras. Plants usually take four years to flower from seed. Offsets are often produced which can be carefully taken off and potted separately. I favour a loam-based compost for these.

Crossandra   T   family *Acanthaceae*

Crossandra infundibuliformis

Crossandra infundibuliformis from semi tropical rain forest in Malaysia and India is the only species normally grown and is well worth acquiring or raising from seed, which can give you a flowering plant in as little as eight months. In the right temperatures flowers are produced almost continuously and the foliage itself is an attractive shiny green. The flowers are orange-red and emerge from the bracts in such a way as to look curiously like half flowers. A very attractive variety, *C. i.* 'Mona Walhed', has salmon-pink flowers and will remain at 30 cm (1 ft) as opposed to growing up to the 60 cm (2 ft) of the species. Seed needs a high temperature of 24–26°C (75–80°F) in March to

83

germinate well. The pest to watch out for is whitefly. Plants will respond to being cut back when they become leggy; resulting growth will either make good cuttings or can be grown on to make a new plant.

Crotalaria W family *Leguminosae*

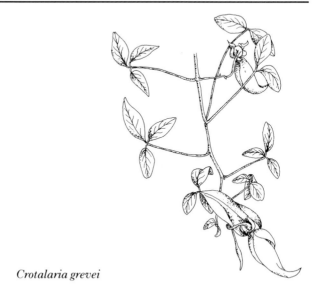

Crotalaria grevei

These are elegant plants with very unusual flowers. I like the origin of their name which derives from *krotalon;* Greek for castanet; this is because the seeds rattle inside the inflated pods. The only species I have grown is *Crotalaria grevei* which has lovely lime-green- and pinky-orange-coloured pea-like flowers some 5 cm (2 in) long. The only problems were that plants became very straggly and needed to be well supported. They were also under constant attack from red spider mite. However, they redeemed themselves by responding extremely well to pruning which I often used to solve both problems. I have seen seed offered of both *C. grevei* and *C. cunninghamii,* an Australian species with green flowers. Cuttings taken during spring and summer root well. Seed should be soaked for two hours before sowing at 18–21°C (65–70°F).

Ctenanthe T family *Marantaceae* Brazil

Cultivation of these is similar to that of their close relation *Calathea*. They will not like cold temperatures or fluctuations and specifically dislike having to sit in wet boggy compost, particularly if it is colder than they like. A peat-based compost and warm humid conditions will be rewarded by a display of very attractive foliage. *Ctenanthe lubbersiana* has 23-cm (9-in) long leaves in many different shades of green. *C. oppenheimiana* 'Tricolor' has longer leaves which are cream and green in bold areas with a pinky-purple underside. Watch out for red spider mite which like to attack these plants especially under dry conditions. When potting, usually in early summer, offsets can be taken from the parent plants. Alternatively shoot cuttings can be taken.

Cuphea   W   family *Lythraceae*

This used to be represented only by *Cuphea ignea,* a Mexican species known as the Cigar Plant because of its cigar-shaped flowers. It is easily raised by seed which will produce neat little plants covered in bright orange flowers within a few months. It is best treated as an annual although it is an evergreen perennial. By the autumn the plants will have become straggly and stopped flowering. It is possible to cut them back but I prefer to throw them away and start afresh the following year. Recently I have noticed *C. hyssopifolia* offered for sale. This makes a small shrubby plant to about 60 cm (2 ft), after which it becomes straggly. The flowers are small, either pink or white and less tube-like than *C. ignea.* Both like good light and will do well either planted in a border or in pots. It is normal to raise fresh batches of *C. ignea* by seed and to propagate *C. hyssopifolia* by cuttings. As it is of a shrubby nature the latter can be kept for longer.

Cupressus   FF/C   family *Pinaceae*

Virtually any *Cupressus* easily raised as a batch from seed can be used as young plants in small pots to add height or backing to a greenhouse display. Particularly suitable is *Cupressus macrocarpa,* the Monterey Cypress, which has very attractive juvenile foliage with a lovely lemon scent when crushed or moved. However, a really choice specimen *Cupressus* would be *C. cashmeriana* known as the Kashmir Cypress although it is probably also from Tibet. In the greenhouse either planted in the border or confined to a pot or tub it makes a most graceful small tree, the branches of which bear sprays of downward sweeping glaucous silvery-blue foliage. Plants are either raised from seed which is probably easier and best sown in spring. It is difficult but not impossible to root cuttings, preferably 'heeled', about 10 cm (4 in) long. I have found that taking these in summer at a temperature of 15°C (60°F) is the best way. As the plants grow and become small trees they will eventually become confined to the largest container you can accommodate sensibly. From then on good watering and liquid feeding is essential with perhaps a top dressing every spring.

Cycads

This group of plants are the most primitive living seed-bearing plants, belonging to the family Cycadaceae. They were around when dinosaurs roamed the earth during the Carboniferous Age some 50 to 60 million years ago at the time when the coal beds were formed. Although they look rather like palms, which are of course flowering plants, they are more closely related to conifers. This is because their seeds are naked and they do not have flowers but cone-like structures instead. Male and female plants exist separately and pollen from the male cone travels to the female cone in the wind. Once pollen has landed in the right area fertilisation takes place, not by the growth of a pollen tube down which the pollen travels to the ovule, but by antherozoids which swim in moisture in much the same way as a fern. This is assisted by the ovule which secretes a drop of fluid at fertilisation; this traps the pollen grain and, as it dries, sucks it in.

Another strange thing about them is their coralloid root masses which appear at the surface of the pot or soil they are planted in. I was amazed when I found out that these contain blue green algae which have a symbiotic (mutually beneficial) relationship with the cycad involving nitrogen fixation like the root nodules of leguminous plants.

Yet another strange feature is that the seeds, which are poisonous, are fully formed at the time of fertilisation. In fact you can usually see them clearly on the female cone. Having been fertilised growth is continuous so you could say that seed has begun to germinate even before it is sown and there is no need to break dormancy. Seeds have a red or yellow outer coating which should be removed after having been soaked for a couple of days. I have sown seed of *Cycas revoluta* successfully but I am afraid it takes some years to grow a plant of appreciable size. This species is probably best able to tolerate cool conditions but as a group they prefer warm or tropical temperatures.

Cycas revoluta from China and the East Indies is perhaps the best known and most often grown cycad and is called the Sago Palm. In recent years they seem to crop up quite frequently in garden centres for a price. I have one which although beautiful has not grown at all in eighteen months. This is quite commonplace. These plants have more character than ordinary plants which grow more or less continuously. Sometimes something will happen to them which will put them into an almighty sulk during which they refuse to grow. During this it is best to humour them by keeping them light and allowing the soil just to dry out between waterings. In this way they will remain healthy until they decide to grow. This is worth waiting for as several new leaves are usually produced at once. *Cycas circinnalis* from the East Indies is beautiful but will grow extremely large particularly in a warm humid atmosphere and is not easy to obtain.

I am pleased to notice *Zamia* species occasionally being offered for sale especially *Z. furfuracea* which is particularly attractive with its brown fuzz all over the surface of the leaves. Although enjoying warmth I have found that high humidity is best avoided. Generally it pays to allow the surface of the compost to become dry between waterings.

Cyclamen   W   family *Primulaceae*   Europe, Mediterranean to Iran

---

The greenhouse Cyclamen is *Cyclamen persicum* with elegant flowers of light or dark pink, sometimes white, which also have a delicate almost peppery scent. However, most of the plants we see today are the result of years of breeding and selection. For a while the popular varieties seemed to get larger and larger with huge blooms and no perfume. Recently the trend seems to be including smaller daintier flowers and I am glad to see that perfume has returned as well. Plants are usually raised in batches from seed. Open pollinated varieties are sown during summer and will flower the winter after next. However, F1 hybrids sown in March will flower the following winter. Seed needs to be dark to germinate at 15°C (60°F). Cover seed by 6 mm ($\frac{1}{4}$ in) after having soaked them for 24 hours. Prick out when the second leaf has appeared. Watering must be done carefully as they will quickly collapse if over- or underwatered. Keep an eye open for vine weevil larvae (see page 32) which hatch in the compost and eat the roots. Although often described as a cool house plant I think they should have a minimum of 10°C (50°F) to do well. In cold conditions they are more prone to overwatering and botrytis (see page 34) which can cause discoloration of the petals. I never used to think that it was worth keeping the corms from one year to the next. This is probably true if a batch is being raised for display work every year. However, I have recently seen magnificent specimens of some age. After flowering allow growth to continue for a while but slow up watering so that all foliage has died down by about June. Keep the dormant corm dry until the end of summer when it can be gradually watered back into growth. Repot occasionally and feed well whilst the plant is building itself up to flower.

Cymbopogon   W   family *Graminae*

The best repellant I know against midges and mosquitos is Citronella oil. I always used to think it was extracted from *Citrus* but it is based on an essential oil which comes from a grass called *Cymbopogon nardus*. A close relative, *C. exultatus* from Western Australia, is rather like a smaller version of pampas grass. It can be raised from seed and will make an attractive greenhouse plant which can tolerate very hot temperatures. Not surprisingly the leaves have a lemon scent when crushed.

87

Cyperus   W   family *Cyperaceae*

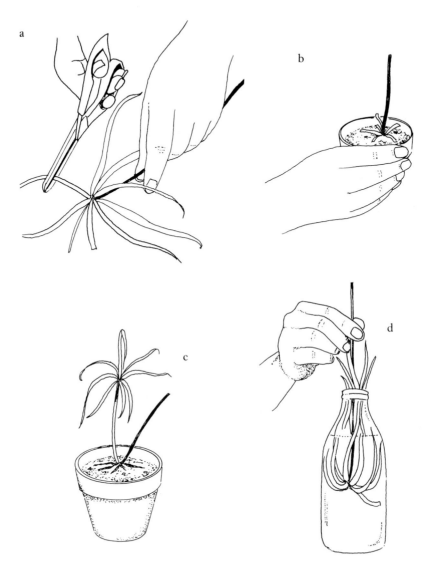

(*a*) If you want several cuttings remove the umbrellas from the plant, trim off the leaves and place them in a jar of water with the stems sticking up. (*b*) Roots will form from the umbrellas. They can then be potted. (*c*) The old umbrella will rot away and new shoots are sent up. (*d*) If you only need one cutting simply put the whole umbrella upside down into a milk bottle of water.

Umbrella plants make effective plantings around indoor ponds, or good pot plants either as specimens or grown as a batch to be used as foliage around more decorative plants. Most commonly grown is *Cyperus alternifolius* from Madagascar. It will grow to a graceful 1.2 m (4 ft) or more. *C. diffusus* is much smaller, about 45 cm (18 in) in height, and has slightly wider leaves and a generally more squat appearance. These two species are very easy to grow, but although they should never dry out it is not essential to have them standing in water. Propagation is either by seed, division or by cuttings. These plants have a way of propagating themselves naturally; the umbrella part of the plant consists of very closely packed leaves on a stem. This growth of leaves will bend down and into the water of their native habitat and in time roots will grow from the nodes around the leaves and stems. A new plant will grow upwards towards the light and air, which, when the old stalk has rotted, will float away to start a new colony. We can use this ability be either cutting off the umbrellas and upending them in water (a milk bottle is ideal), or the umbrellas can be cut off with a small length of stem attached, the leaves are trimmed and the cutting inserted upside down into cutting compost with the stalk sticking up in the air.

C. papyrus is the plant from which the ancient Egyptians made their writing paper of the same name. A tall plant of 3 m (10 ft) it is extremely showy and graceful. However, it needs tropical conditions to do well. All the best specimens I have seen have been planted by tropical pools and not actually in the water. Seed or division are the best methods of propagating this one.

Cyphomandra   W   family *Solanaceae*   South America

Cyphomandra betacea, the Tree Tomato from Brazil, is an interesting plant to grow from seed as it can produce fruit in its second year. These are attractive and are like egg-shaped tomatoes which are mottled green and red before turning red. They are supposed to have the flavour of a tomato but I have found them to be disappointing when eaten raw. Perhaps tree tomato chutney would be an improvement. You will need some space to grow this as it can reach 4 m (12 ft). It is better to train a branching plant by pinching out the tips of the growths. This way it should fruit as a smaller plant. The leaves are large, soft and rather prone to attack by whitefly.

Datura   W   family *Solanaceae*

The only thing that prevents me from describing these plants as being excellent is their tendency to suffer from attacks by red spider mite and whitefly which seem to take it in turns to spoil one's enjoyment of growing them. The only cultural advice I can give to ward them off is to thoroughly and vigorously spray the plants with water, especially the undersides of the leaves, as many times a day as is feasible during the hot dry spells when attacks are most likely to occur. *Datura sanguinea* is a delightful if rather large species which will reach 2 m (6 ft) and is best pruned very hard each year after flowering. From Peru, it produces long orange-red flowers during summer. *D. suaveolens,* also from Peru, is the true Angels Trumpet with its large white scented flowers. A good small plant is *D. metel* 'Golden Queen' which will flower when small during its first year from seed. Flowers are a glorious fragrant double yellow trumpet very freely produced during summer. All these can be grown easily from seed. Subsequent propagation can be by cuttings of half ripe wood in May. Given a temperature of 24°C (75°F) they will root within three weeks. Fortunately *Datura* respond well to hard pruning, which in older specimens can go right back into the old wood. It is necessary to prune all of them in the autumn. Not only does this get rid of pest eggs but keeps the plants compact.

A word of warning is that these plants are known for having poisonous, narcotic and medicinal properties and are to be treated with respect. The first experience I had with *Datura* was when a colleague inadvertently wiped sap into one of her eyes. It had the effect of dilating the pupil which looked very odd when the other was contracted against the light. It was only after puzzling a few doctors that we remembered the *Datura sanguinea* she had been pruning. The effect wore off after a day.

Desfontainea   FF   family *Loganiaceae*   Chile

There is only one species, *Desfontainea spinosa.* Hardiness of this attractive evergreen is dubious in most areas which is why it makes a good little shrub for a frost free house. It likes to be well ventilated in winter, cool and shaded in summer. Give it these conditions and you will be rewarded with tube-like red and yellow flowers in summer. If seed is obtainable this is probably easier than cuttings which should be taken in August about 8 cm (3 in) long.

Dianella   C   family *Liliaceae*   E Asia, Polynesia, Australia

---

These are the Flax Lilies which although not wildly exciting to grow are worth trying for their interesting form and blue berries produced after rather insignificant flowers. *Dianella tasmanica* will make a clump of 1.5 m (5 ft), whereas *D. caerulea,* the Paroo Lily, will only reach 60 cm (2 ft) in height. They like to be shaded and kept moist in summer otherwise some leaves and tips of leaves will go brown which spoils the whole appearance of the plant.

Similarly, although they will tolerate frost free conditions their appearance is not improved by cold weather. Both these species produce their berries in autumn. Propagation is by seed sown at 18–21°C (65–70°F), or by division.

Dichorisandra   T   family *Commelinaceae*   Tropical America

---

These are closely related to *Tradescantia* and are like giant, mostly upright versions of them. A little difficult to obtain they make lovely plants as the flowers and foliage are attractive. *Dichorisandra thyrsiflora* from Brazil grows to 1.2 m (4 ft) in height, the stems bearing deep green sheathing leaves. The flowers which are mostly borne in summer and autumn are a dark intense blue with bright yellow anthers. *D. reginae* is smaller with leaves attractively marked with silver. *D. mosaica* has dark roundish green leaves the surfaces of which are traced with white lines and have reddish-purple undersides. The flower, produced in autumn, is clear blue with yellow anthers. They must have tropical conditions to do anything other than survive although plants can be kept cooler and drier during winter. Peat-based compost is preferable. Propagation is easily carried out by division or cuttings. Seed can be germinated at 21–24°C (70–75°F).

Dichroa   FF/C   family *Saxifragaceae*   E Asia

The only species in cultivation is *Dichroa febrifuga* which is an unusual plant resembling *Hydrangea* to which it is related. Coming mainly from the Himalayas it is only hardy in the mildest areas and really needs a frost free or cool house. It is an evergreen shrub with heads of flowers which appear to be blue, pink and white at the same time. These are borne towards the end of the summer and are followed by small deep blue berries. It is more likely that one will find seed for sale than a plant. Having grown a plant it can then be propagated easily by shoot tip cuttings.

Dieffenbachia   T   family *Araceae*   Tropical America

The first mention of these plants must be a warning that all parts of the plant are poisonous. If the sap is eaten it will cause inflammation of mouth and throat resulting in difficulty of speech, hence the plant's common name of Dumb Cane. In practical terms this means keeping plants away from the reach of children and never eating while taking cuttings or handling the plants. Do not let this put you off growing these beautiful foliage plants as a group of these in

91

a tropical house are delightful. They will not like lower temperatures and leaves will go limp and yellow if they are subjected to them for any length of time. There are many species and varieties available which all need the same warm humid treatment. My favourite is *Dieffenbachia* × *bausei* which has a narrower leaf than *D. picta* and a lot of spots and blotches of white and dark green on a yellowish-green background. Plants frequently produce strange flowers when they are happy. These have the typical spathe and spadix structure common to all plants in the family.

If a plant is becoming too tall and has shed a few lower leaves new plants can be made by taking stem cuttings (see page 22). The shoot tip or tips can be used as 8-cm (3-in) cuttings in the normal way. The stem can then be cut into sections each containing at least two nodes. These should be laid down into a tray of cutting compost so that they are half buried beneath the soil. Keep these moist and at a temperature of 21–24°C (70–75°F) and they will root and send up new shoots when they can be potted. The stump of the old plant cut down to within 5–8 cm (2–3 in) of the soil will produce new shoots if kept warm, light and not too wet. This entire operation is best carried out in late spring unless very good heat and lighting is available. Seed is rarely sown but must be fresh; older than two months will be of little use. Bury seed by 1.2 cm ($\frac{1}{2}$ in) at a temperature of 24–26°C (75–80°F). Plants prefer a peat-based compost.

Dioscorea   T   family *Dioscoreaceae*

Dioscorea discolor from Surinam is the species mostly grown for its ornamental foliage. Leaves are heart-shaped and marked with pale green and silvery-grey over a dark green background. Undersides of the leaves are a luminous maroon. The plant is twining and makes so much growth in a season that it is hard to believe that it dies down in autumn and will make all that growth again from the following spring. It is related to the Yam and has underground storage tubers. For this reason the plant should be kept dry after it has died down and only watered again very carefully at first from February onwards. Propagation is by removing small tubers in the spring and growing them individually. I have found that if plants are left in the same pot they become very poor. It is best to repot every other year just as they start to shoot in the spring. A peaty compost with some loam is the best—and remember to put a tall tripod of canes in early as this plant really will romp away.

Dizygotheca W/T   family *Araliaceae*   Australasia

Only one species is commonly grown and this is *Dizygotheca elegantissima* from the New Hebrides. The shape of the leaves really is elegant; they are very dark green and divided into narrow toothed leaflets radiating out from the leaf

Brunfelsia calycina
'Macrantha'
(right)

Aeonium arboreum
'Atropurpureum'
(below left)

Anthurium
andreanum
(below right)

Begonia cheimantha
'Love Me' is a
fibrous-rooted hybrid
(left)

Celosia
'Fairy Fountains'
(below)

Callistemon citrinus
var. 'Splendens'
(above left)

Camellia reticulata
'Butterfly Wings'
(above right)

Grevillea banksii
(right)

Haemanthus multiflorus
(above)

A selection of Trumpet
Pitcher Plants:
Sarracenia × *catesbaei*,
S. purpurea and *S. flava*
(left)

stalk. Although growing much stronger and faster in warmer temperatures it is possible to grow them at 10°C (50°F) but they will require less water, especially in winter, and will become very squat and smaller leaved, almost like a dwarf form. Plants are easily raised from seed sown in April at 24–26°C (75–80°F) and placed in the light. If several seedling plants the same size are available it is a good idea to pot them three to a pot of peat-based compost to make a really good display. I have never known plants to be raised by cuttings.

Dombeya   W   family *Sterculiaceae*   Tropical Africa/Madagascar

---

Even *Dombeya × cayeuxii,* although capable of reaching 6 m (20 ft) tall, is well mannered enough to produce its drooping heads of powder pink flowers when only small enabling it to be grown in pots, successive batches being raised from cuttings. Planted out this large plant can be pruned regularly to obtain the height required. This is best done by training a stem and then pollarding after flowering at the end of summer. It does make an ugly plant when this operation has just been carried out but shoots and large soft furry leaves will quickly grow to make a new head. I always wear an overall and goggles when pruning a tall plant. If you are working under the head of the plant hairs fall off the leaves and stems and are extremely itchy. This is a hybrid between *D. wallichii* and *D. burgessiae* and is very showy. However, *D. burgessiae* is worth growing and is easier, only reaching 2 m (6 ft) under glass. Flowers are white with pink suffusing outwards in veins from the centre and are produced between August and December. Pruning after flowering consists of thinning out older shoots by cutting them right back to within a few buds of the base or of older wood. I should use a loam-based compost especially in pots as they will require a lot of watering and food in summer, and being large plants will be more stable in a heavier compost.

Doxantha   W   family *Bignoniaceae*   Tropical America/W Indies

---

Doxantha unguis-cati, the Cats Claw *Bignonia,* is an unusual but spectacular climber which although it comes from tropical places will do well enough in a warm house. It flowers early in the year, producing bright golden-yellow flowers all over the large twining form of the plant. It needs a lot of head room to climb, securing itself with hooked tendrils as it goes. Plants do better if planted into the floor of the house rather than in pots. After flowering it can be cut back to a smaller area otherwise it will become very invasive. Should it be necessary to prune back to within a few nodes of the base it will respond well to this treatment and will be of flowering size again after a season's growth. Propagation can either be by cuttings of short growths if you can find them or pieces of long growths if not. It is worth trying semi ripe material from the middle of a stem cutting below a node at the base and above at the top. Sometimes, if planted out, suckers will be formed around the base which can be dug up carefully and potted or transplanted.

Dracaena C/W   family *Liliaceae*

A large and versatile group of plants, they prefer a minimum of 15°C (60°F) but are still worth growing in warm conditions. *Dracaena deremensis* varieties are among the most attractive. They will reach 1.2 m (4 ft) in height before becoming leggy and unattractive. The leaves are all deep green in the species but there is a wide white stripe down the middle of the leaf in *D. d.* 'Bausei' and two stripes in *D. d.* '*Warneckei*'. *D. d.* 'Souvenir de Augustus Shryer' has leaves edged with creamy bands. *D. marginata* from Madagascar can reach heights of 3 m (10 ft) but becomes very bare at the bottom of the stem. *D. m.* 'Tricolor' is particularly attractive, the narrow leaves being striped with cream, pink and green. *D. draco* is the Dragon Tree which is endemic to the Canary Islands. Although natural sources of this are quite rare it is commonly found in cultivation. This one can withstand cool conditions. More difficult to grow is *D. sanderiana* which is the Ribbon Plant from Cameroon. Growing to 90 cm (3 ft) it is more upright and in less of a rosette than the others. *D. godseffiana* is also more difficult. In structure it is more informal than the others. A speckling of creamy-yellow over the leaves gives it the name of Gold-Dust *Dracaena*.

Propagation is usually by sections of stem each with at least two nodes and about 2.5–5 cm (1–2 in) long. These should be laid on some cutting compost either upright or horizontal but with some stem under the surface. Kept moist and warm they will produce roots and shoots. It is possible to obtain plants as stems or 'logs'. These are usually waxed at either end. Scrape off the wax on the bottom and stand it in water until roots appear. Once the roots are growing the 'log' can be potted and a shoot will grow out and develop into a plant. Seed can also be sown in March at 24–26°C (75–80°F).

Echium C   family *Boraginaceae*   Mediterranean/Canary Islands

---

There are some hardy species but the larger ones are not dependable even in milder districts. The Abbey Gardens on Tresco in the Scilly Isles usually has some magnificent specimens growing outside and even has some varieties of its own. Most commonly grown in the greenhouse is *Echium wildprettii,* a hairy biennial from the Canary Islands which is by no means easy to keep healthy. During the winter they have a tendency to rot if even slightly too damp. They like cool dry airy conditions and just enough water to survive on. However, if you are successful in nursing them through the winter you will be rewarded by a spike of pale red flowers which will elevate the total height of the plant to 1.2 m (4 ft). Seed is readily produced and can be collected for a succession of sowings every year. Sow the seed in March or April at a temperature of 15–18°C (60–65°F). *E. fastuosum* is a compact perennial from the Canaries known as the Pride of Madeira. The hairy leaves are an attractive soft white and the flowers are deep blue. *E. pininana* has a very tall flower spike reaching to 4 m (12 ft) when planted out in a cool house border. The spike is full of small blue flowers and is an impressive sight.

Eichhornia C/W/T family *Pontederiaceae* America

Eichhornia crassipes is the Water Hyacinth which has become a menace in tropical waterways, clogging the surface of the water and spreading into a thick mat by way of its rhizomes. It is a pity that these plants are shy of flowering in captivity as they are a beautiful azure blue. How it behaves will depend on the temperature and whether or not it is floating. Floating plants have very inflated petioles (leaf stalks) and long deep purple roots which fish love to lay their eggs in. However, if the plants are growing close to the edge of water and can root into the side the petioles are longer and thinner. Although it is perfectly possible to grow this plant outside during summer and on cooler ponds indoors it will never take off and spread itself into the dense mat that encourages flowering unless it is growing on a tropical pool. If the temperature of the greenhouse is below 4°C (40°F) in winter I would pot the plant up into a well-drained loam compost to overwinter.

Episcia W family *Gesneriaceae* Tropical America

The most commonly grown species is *Episcia dianthiflora*, the Lace Flower, which makes an extremely attractive hanging basket plant with its furry green leaves and strange wispy white flowers. *E. cupreata*, the Flame Violet, makes more of a carpet or mat of growth. The leaves are attractively striped with silver along the veins and the bright red flowers look well against the foliage. Both of these in common with others in the family hate water on their leaves and carelessness in this department will leave scorch marks. Plants are easily raised by seed or cuttings which should be 8 cm (3 in) long. Seeds of *Episcia* hybrids are available. Seed is very fine and is best sown on the surface of peat-based compost, covered with plastic film to keep moisture in and given a temperature of 24–26°C (75–80°F).

Erica C family *Ericaceae*

Erica canaliculata

Cool house Ericas are known as the Cape Heaths as most of them originate from South Africa. They are delightful small autumn and winter flowering shrubs which will do well if kept cool and moist never allowing the compost to become dry. They dislike lime so when potting choose a lime-free peat-based compost with plenty of sharp sand. During summer they can be temporarily moved to a cool shady spot outside. Most commonly grown is *Erica × hyemalis*. This has very fine lime-green foliage and quite large bell-shaped flowers of pink and white. Although it tends to be sold as a houseplant which is discarded after flowering, there are distinct benefits in adding it to a greenhouse display; flowers will last longer and with care the plant can be grown on from year to year in the cooler atmosphere. *E. gracilis* has rosy-red flowers although there is a white flowered form. This will grow to 45 cm (18 in) tall. *E. pageana* is a tall shrub of 1–1.2 m (3–4 ft). It produces bell-shaped yellow flowers during autumn. My favourite is *E. canaliculata* which is another tall one with pure white or occasionally pinkish flowers and black stamens.

The species with soft shoots should be cut back after flowering each year. The shrubbier woodier species however, do not respond so well to pruning and are best left. Seed sown during spring in a peat-based seed compost takes at least a month to germinate and must have light. It is a good idea to incorporate some soil from where heathers grow naturally into their compost at potting up time. Cuttings 2.5–5 cm (1–2 in) long of lateral growths from near the base of the shoots can be taken in summer.

Eriobotrya   C   family *Rosaceae*   East Asia

Eriobotrya japonica is the Japanese Loquat which will grow to 6 m (20 ft) in its natural habitat, producing the edible yellow pear-shaped fruits. However, in the cool house I have never known specimens to bear fruit. They are still worth growing for their large showy toothed leaves which are covered with silvery hair when young. They are extremely easy to grow and make imposing specimens in pots. If you can find the fruit for sale each will contain a large seed. These are best soaked for 24 hours prior to sowing at 10°C (50°F). The important point is not to overwater the compost, which should be well-drained, while the seed is germinating, which will take up to two months.

Erythrina   FF   family *Leguminosae*

Erythrina crista-galli is the Coral Tree from Brazil. It is almost hardy if grown in a sheltered border. After it produces its spectacular red claw-shaped flowers in autumn it will die back for the winter to a tough root stock. Keep plants dry during winter and water gradually in spring as they produce buds which will develop into shoots. These shoots become 2–2.5 m (6–8 ft) tall and will need staking before they flower (watch out for the thorns). Be on guard against red spider mite. The best method of propagation is by seed soaked for 24 hours before being sown in spring. Cuttings can be taken but it is hard to find the right material. The best material would be young shoots 8 cm (3 in) long, with a small heel, pulled off the rootstock.

Eucalyptus   C   family *Myrtaceae*   mostly Australia

Of course many Eucalypts are hardy outside but the interesting thing about them is that their juvenile foliage is frequently very different from the adult. It is for their foliage that many species are grown in pots for the greenhouse and have wide uses as ornamental foliage plants. *Eucalyptus citriodora* is a nice species to try as its leaves have a strong lemon scent. *E. globulus,* the Blue Gum, has very attractive glaucous silver foliage; *E. gunnii,* the Cider Gum, is well known for its silver-blue leaves; *E. niphophila,* the Snow Gum, is worth a try and has elegant foliage which is extremely long lasting when cut. *E. forrestiana* is the only one I would recommend anyone tried as a flowering plant in a pot; called the Fuchsia Gum the bright red fruit pods resemble *Fuchsia* flowers as they hang down. It will still need a large pot and to attain some height before flowering. Seed germinates freely and is best sown in spring. When plants have become too tall they can be cut down drastically or 'stooled'. They will produce

97

bushy growth from the cut which may make them too space-consuming for a small greenhouse. It may be worth keeping one plant just to use for cut foliage all year round.

Eucharis   T   family *Amaryllidaceae*   Colombia

These are tropical bulbs which should be planted several to a pot in spring into peat-based compost. If there is no foliage the tip of the bulb should be just above the surface. A temperature of 21°C (70°F) is needed for these to get going well, and thereafter at least 18°C (65°F). When growing well there should be two or three lots of flowers produced annually and they really are worth striving for. Flowers are large, white and vaguely *Narcissus*-like with a delightful sweet scent. While temperatures are up to optimum water freely except for a short period in autumn. I have found it best not to dry them out completely between flowering unless temperatures have to drop. *Eucharis amazonica (E. grandiflora)* is the Amazon Lily and the most often grown. Propagation is either by offsets removed in spring or by seed sown as soon as ripe.

Eucomis   FF   family *Liliaceae*   S and Tropical Africa

Most of these can really be grown outside in a sheltered border but I had to include them as the pineapple flowers are a great favourite of mine. Having invested in the bulbs I certainly would not leave their fate to chance outside during winter in my garden which has no particularly sheltered bed. They are all grown in pots and moved indoors. For a frost free or cool greenhouse clumps of these planted out in well-drained loam or potted in a loam-based compost would be delightful. *Eucomis bicolor,* the most available, grows to 60 cm (2 ft) in height and by midsummer produces a spike of long-lasting star-shaped flowers of green edged with purple. Above these is a tuft of leaves giving the whole spike the appearance of a pineapple. Even the stem is attractively spotted with deep maroon. The whole plant dies down in autumn and should be kept dry during winter until growth appears the following spring. Other species should be treated in the same way. *E. zambesiaca* is the exception as it is more tropical and needs a much warmer greenhouse.

Euphorbia   C/W   family *Euphorbiaceae*

The most well known of these must be *Euphorbia pulcherrima* more familiar as the Poinsettia sold in their thousands in Britain at Christmas time and loved for their red, white or pink bracts. If you look closely in the centre of the bracts you will see the more insignificant true flowers. These familiar plants descend from tall shrubby plants native to Mexico. On visits to the warmer parts of the world much taller plants can be seen than those grown in Britain. Most of our plants are smaller growing strains that have also been dwarfed by the use of hormones before we buy them. This is why if you successfully keep a plant going it will seem to grow on a much larger scale than before.

A group of these plants makes a superb seasonal display for a greenhouse or conservatory but they need a minimum winter temperature of 13°C (55°F) to do well. After flowering cut off the dead bracts and allow the plants to become almost dry. After a month of this treatment (usually by April) plants can be pruned hard and watered to make them grow again. Repotting takes place now, or at least a top dressing. Retain the five best stems that sprout from the base and water and feed well throughout summer. Then comes the tricky bit which is getting them to produce their coloured bracts again; they need short days to do this. If your greenhouse is not affected by any unnatural light (including faint light from a street lamp) they will turn red naturally. However, if any artificial light does reach them you will have to set up a blacking out regime to give them no less than 14 hours of uninterruped darkness per day. This should begin towards the end of September and continue for eight weeks. Black polythene can be used effectively for this but it must be removed daily to allow light in for the rest of the time. Cuttings can be taken of the shoots made by the plants after pruning. When you remove these you will see that they bleed white sap. Dipping them in water will stop this. I avoid hormone rooting treatments as sometimes these seem to burn the end of the cutting. I also root them singly in small pots as they dislike root disturbance at potting up time. It is important not to overwater these plants at any stage.

E. fulgens is an attractive shrubby little species with small scarlet-orange bracts. They are grown in a similar way to the Poinsettia but need warmer treatment. They are occasionally sold as cut flowers. If you buy the stems of bracts you will probably be able to find good cutting material on them. *E. millii (E. splendens)* is the Crown of Thorns and is a succulent species with spiky stems and red bracts. There are also varieties which are yellow or pink. This has its origins in Madagascar and is just hardy enough to survive in the cool house along with other succulent Euphorbia.

Euryops   C   family *Compositae*   Africa

Euryops pectinatus is a most attractive shrub which is almost continuously in flower. The silver-white leaves covered with down are closely crowded together to give a lovely compact appearance and the rich yellow daisy-like flowers are freely produced and held away from the rest of the plant by long 13-cm (5-in) stalks. It is very easy to grow and propagate by cuttings. When it does stop flowering this is a good time to prune it back to restrict size. This is a good plant for pots or planting into the border. Even very small plants will flower.

× **Fatshedera**   FF/C   family *Araliaceae*

This is a hybrid between *Fatsia* and *Hedera*. × *Fatshedera lizei* or Fat Headed Lizzie can be trained either as a bush by stopping the plant close to the base or as a tall plant which will need support. The variegated form is quite attractive but I would consider this to be of more use as a houseplant than taking up valuable space in the greenhouse. One unusual use I once saw it put to was as a stock plant on which to graft unusual Ivy varieties. A tall × *Fatshedera* was decapitated at a height of 1.2 m (4 ft) and four small ivy shoots were grafted into the cut surface; in time these trailed down their borrowed stem rather effectively. As it is a hybrid no seed is produced and propagation is by cuttings. Not only the tip will root, but sections of stem bearing nodes can also be rooted.

Fatsia   FF/C   family *Araliaceae*

Fatsia japonica, a native of Japan and Taiwan, shares the common name of Castor Oil Plant with *Ricinus*. It is hardy in most areas but is a useful foliage plant for the frost free or cool house and has an attractive variegated form. It is easily raised from seed sown in spring and produces heads of creamy flowers during winter. *F. papyrifera (Tetrapanax papyrifera)* is the plant from which Chinese rice paper is made from pith inside the shoots. It is well worth growing from seed and makes a tall plant with large silver-grey felt-covered leaves which are a furry orange-green when young. Not a plant for the small greenhouse if you want room for other plants as well.

Feijoa   FF   family *Myrtaceae*   Brazil

I like *Feijoa sellowiana,* but this shrub never does well for me outside, although it can survive well on a south wall. It makes a good greenhouse plant with rounded greyish leaves which are white beneath. The petals of the flowers, which are borne in late spring inside, are red at the centre and white on the outside. They are complemented by a brush of showy red stamens with yellow anthers. The fruit is edible as are, apparently, the petals although I have never tried them. Propagation is by seed, which should be rinsed well three times before sowing to wash away any inhibitors, or by cuttings.

100

Ferns

True ferns are spore-bearing plants and should not be confused with flowering plants such as *Asparagus,* which may well be fern-like in appearance but are only too often referred to as ferns. The uses of ferns in the greenhouse are many. They are attractive as specimens in their own right, and make excellent foils for flowering plants, particularly orchids, which although they might have spectacular flowers often have less than attractive leaves and stems. Ferns that grow epiphytically can be tied on to bark and grown alongside orchids and bromeliads to give very effective displays.

Cultivation Ferns can be ridiculously easy or maddeningly difficult to grow. They love humidity and a shady place but hate dryness in the air or at the roots. Direct sun will scorch and yellow them. It is infuriating to find wonderful specimens that have grown themselves from spores under the staging while those in pots receiving all the attention die off. Close attention to shading will always pay dividends.

Although most ferns will grow adequately in an average peat-based compost they prefer a more open mixture. I have found the addition of coarse peat and perlite beneficial. It is not good for them to become too potbound not so much because of the crowding but they are far more likely to dry out. Some which form clumps can be divided and repotted to give new plants. For spore sowing see page 17.

A Selection of Ferns *Adiantum* are the delicate Maidenhair Ferns. *A. capillus-veneris* is the commonest with light green fronds on wiry black stems. *A. raddianum* is more robust. The variety 'Fritz Leuthii' is often grown. It is very compact, the fronds being bluish-green. There are many other species but few are available. My favourite is *A. trapeziforme* which has large angular pinnae on its fronds. It is worth looking for it in botanical collections. All are extremely intolerant of dry air.

Asplenium are able to withstand some dry air. There are only two species widely available and both are well worth growing. The cool-loving species is *A. bulbiferum* from New Zealand, Australia and India. A very graceful fern it will reach 90 cm (3 ft) round. It produces bulbils or plantlets along its older fronds (see page 25 for propagation). *A. nidus,* the Bird's Nest Fern, is very different having great strapping fronds coming from a central part that is hairy and resembles a bird's nest. I remember the fern professor at Kew Gardens using a frond as a mask at a fancy dress party. This fern will withstand lower temperatures but needs a minimum of 13°C (55°F) preferably higher to do well. In tropical conditions growth will be very fast and lush. One thing they do not like is uneven watering. This results in new fronds stopping and starting which causes ugly distorted growth. Slugs can be a problem, especially with new growth. Both plants like an open peaty compost.

101

Adiantum raddianum

Nephrolepis are the popular Ladder or Boston Ferns. The species usually grown is *N. exaltata* and its varieties. Good for either pots or hanging baskets they are graceful and relatively easy to grow. They like perhaps a little more light than other ferns but must have a moist atmosphere. Some plants will send out furry runners from the main rhizomes that make up their root structure. Small plants will form at the ends of these which is why they are so good for hanging baskets when they will sometimes make a complete ball of growth. These small runners can also be used for propagation.

Pellaea rotundifolia from New Zealand and the Norfolk Islands is the Button Fern which has dark green rounded pinnae on its fronds. It can tolerate cool temperatures but is consistent in its dislike of dry air or any kind of drying out at the roots.

If you have space in your greenhouse try growing a tree fern. *Dicksonia antarctica* from Australia is amongst the commonest grown and can withstand cool conditions easily. Even from spores a fair sized fern can be had in four or five years. Given time they will, of course, become very large as they grow up to 9 m (30 ft) in the wild. A smaller choice would be *Blechnum gibbum* which has a dark rosette of fronds on top of a 90-cm (3-ft) tall black trunk.

Epiphytic ferns are difficult to control in pots as they seem to spend all their time trying to escape from them by sending out creeping rhizomes which in their turn will bear fronds. *Davallia* falls into this category. *D. canariensis* from the W Mediterranean is the Hare's Foot Fern as the rootstock is covered in brown fur. Very similar are *D. solida fijiensis* and *D. trichomanoides* from Malaya. I have used these very effectively on bromeliad logs. They are a little more versatile than most ferns as they can tolerate a certain amount of dry air. Sections of creeping rhizome can be used as cuttings, 5–8 cm (2–3 in) long,

Davallia canariensis

with fronds attached. These should be laid down on to the compost and nestled into it. Cover the cuttings, as humidity and warmth will help them to grow their own roots.

Another similar epiphyte is *Polypodium aureum* although this one operates on a much larger scale to *Davallia* and is most difficult to keep within a pot. I would say it is only worth growing as an epiphyte by giving it a piece of dead tree or bark to cling to. Even in a hanging basket it seems to suffer from claustrophobia and needs to escape. Otherwise it is extremely attractive especially *P. a.* 'Mandaianum' which has a glaucous bluish-green appearance.

Platycerium is a different sort of epiphyte as it does not have the creeping rhizomes. It does have infertile fronds which make the shield-like clasping part at the centre and fertile fronds which spread out and hang in such a way as to give it the name of Stag's Horn Fern. I have always loved these. The commonest is *P. bifurcatum* from Australia so called because of the way the fertile fronds bifurcate into two parts at the end. The most impressive must be *P. grande* from Malaya and N Australia which really does make a massive plant. It is possible to grow these in pots but far better specimens will be had by binding them on to boards with a lump of Osmunda fibre at the back. They can then be fixed up high to be admired. Eventually they will form a colony of their own and be supported by their own rotting infertile fronds which will hold moisture. Watering is something of an art as they will certainly not appreciate being overwatered but will begin to suffer and look shrivelled if underwatered. Liquid feeding is essential in summer as they have no compost from which to extract food, although to an extent they will derive some from their own rotting fronds. They produce spores on the undersides of the end of the fertile fronds which can be tapped on to paper when ripe and sown (see page 17).

103

There are two water ferns worth a mention which look similar to large duckweed at first glance. *Salvinia natans* is very pretty and can be floated on the surface of an indoor pond or tank provided the temperature is warm or tropical. It has no true roots but strange divided leaves that do the same job. It is easy to keep in summer but the old plant dies off in winter leaving spores produced from sporangia on the lower surfaces. It is best to overwinter them in a pan half filled with loamy compost and topped up with water. If a few plants are floated on this before winter hopefully they will shed their spores which can be stored cool or warm in the loam until spring, when they should germinate, provided the loam has not been allowed to dry out. *Azolla caroliniana* is very similar and both are in the family Salviniaceae.

Ficus   W   family *Moraceae*

This is a very versatile group of plants, containing as it does species with such a variety of habit. One of the best known must be *Ficus elastica* the Rubber Plant from tropical Asia. Not, perhaps, for the small greenhouse, a group of these is an impressive sight in a large house or conservatory. *F. e.* 'Decora' is the bolder, sturdier variety usually seen. In addition there are several different coloured varieties. *F. e.* 'Black Prince' is a lovely dark leafed plant. One of the most striking is *F. e.* 'Zulu Shield' with very bold markings of pink, cream and greens. When plants become too large a whole new batch can be raised from one plant. The tip can be used in the usual way, but in addition each node with a leaf can be used as a cutting. Cuts should be made just above the leaf and 2.5 cm (1 in) below. The leaf should be curled round and tied with an elastic band and the stem pushed into a pot of cutting compost with the whole cutting being held in place by the leaf being tied to a small cane. Kept warm and moist the cutting will root and the shoot in the axil of leaf and stem will grow to make a new plant. It is important to have the shoot pointing upwards when the cutting is inserted. Having made as many cuttings as possible from reasonably soft stem, the whole of the remainder can be cut back hard and new shoots will develop from the stump. If you are afraid to tackle all this they can also be air layered (see page 27).

   F. benghalensis is the Banyan of India and tropical Africa. The stems, shoots and undersides of the leaves of this large growing, branching plant are covered with russet hairs. Although it is at its best in warm and tropical conditions it will survive well in a cool house. *F. benjamina* from India is the familiar Weeping Fig which becomes a large tree in its native habitat. Even in the warm greenhouse it will become very tall if planted out. Vigilance is necessary to prevent scale insects from becoming a problem. Many a fine specimen has been ruined by the stickiness and sooty mould resulting from such attacks. In recent years there have been some fine varieties of this species produced with good variegated leaves and a smaller habit. *F. diversifolia (F. deltoidea)* is the attractive Mistletoe Fig from India and Malaya. It is a strange thing with the Figs that you never see them flower. They do this secretly in a receptacle hidden by scales. This species bears small inedible yellow fruit all year round which is its chief attraction. It is also a manageable size, usually within 90 cm (3 ft). From China and Japan comes a small trailing species, *F. pumila (F. repens)* or Creeping Fig. This has small round leaves and will either trail over a pot or will climb. If left to its own devices it often climbs up glass walls fixing itself with clinging roots as it goes. There are various varieties with variegated leaves, variegated margins of the leaf, very small leaves and crinkly leaves. *F. religiosa* is the Peepul or Bo Tree of the Hindus and hails from the East Indies. I have never found it easy to get going. It seems to need a lot of heat to do little more than exist. However, it is worth trying for its unusual heart-shaped leaves which tail off to a fine point. As well as propagating easily from cuttings seed of the *Ficus* should be easy to germinate and sizeable plants can be raised within a year.

Fittonia   T   family *Acanthaceae*   Peru

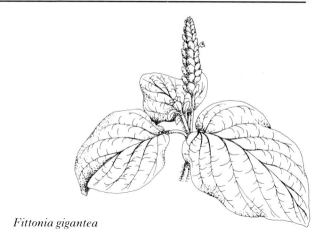

Fittonia gigantea

These are excellent little plants with shallow root systems which need tropical conditions to do well. If asked to grow at lower temperatures extreme care must be taken with watering or they tend to rot. I find that several small plants or well-rooted cuttings planted into a pan of peat-based compost make a fine display for the edge of the staging. There are two main species grown; *Fittonia gigantea* has green leaves netted with red veins. When it is growing well it produces spikes of small pale yellow flowers. *F. verschaffeltii argyroneura* has green leaves netted with silver but the small leafed form *F. v. a.* 'Minima' is more often seen. Five to eight-cm (2–3-in) long cuttings root easily and are best pinched out just after potting to encourage a bushy plant.

Freesia   C   family *Iridaceae*

The plants we all know as Freesias originate from a cross made between two species at Kew Gardens in 1898. The best way to grow them is by planting the corms 5–8 cm (2–3 in) apart and 2.5 cm (1 in) under the surface in loam-based compost in September. Initially they should be kept in a cold frame until they begin to shoot. If it becomes extremely cold they should be moved inside but otherwise covering the frame lights with hessian or other insulation should be sufficient. They should also be given as much air as possible. The next important thing is to get stakes or twigs in them in good time before they have a chance to flop which will do them no good at all. After flowering it is important to look after them well as far as watering and feeding them goes, as this is your investment towards next year's flowers. Move them outside during summer and withhold water when they begin to die down. From this time until they are started again they should be kept dry but in a light position. Smaller corms which come off the plants at potting time can be potted separately and grown on until flowering size. Seed which has been soaked for 24 hours can be sown at 10–15°C (50–60°F).

Fremontodendron   FF   family *Sterculiaceae*   SW USA and Mexico

Fremontodendron californicum is the species normally grown as a tender wall shrub outside. However, it makes an extremely good climber for the frost free house and will do much better with the added protection. Unpruned and planted out it will reach 4.5 m (15 ft) or more but smaller shrubs will flower well in pots. During spring the plant is covered with bright yellow flowers. After this first flush further flowers are produced and flowering will continue sporadically for the rest of the season. The semi evergreen nature of the plant guarantees that most of the attractive lobed hairy leaves will remain on the plant in winter under glass. This plant is easily raised from seed sown in spring at 18°C (65°F). Germination takes four to six weeks. Alternatively, cuttings 8–10 cm (3–4 in) long can be taken during summer. *F.* 'Californian Glory' is worth looking out for. It is a cross between *F. californicum* and *F. mexicanum* and has larger more richly coloured very plentiful blooms.

Fuchsia   C/W   family *Onagraceae*

The *Fuchsias* we grow today were originally derived from several species and are the result of much hybridisation. They make super display plants for the greenhouse and varieties can be chosen that are suitable for growing as bushy

plants, trailers for baskets or very upright growing types which can be trained
as standards or pyramids. Culture is extremely easy; to get really big plants
cuttings should be taken from stock plants towards the end of summer. These
root very quickly if kept moist and humid. If it is impossible to find non-flower-
ing material, remove as many flowers and buds as possible from the cutting
which should be 8 cm (3 in) long. Grow these on in warm conditions
throughout the winter so that they reach their final pots by spring. Large
display plants in 18- or 23-cm (7- or 9-in) pots can be achieved in this way.
Even reasonably large standards can be grown in one year. However, if only
cool or even frost free conditions are available it is best to keep the stock plants
almost dry and cool throughout winter and take the cuttings in spring; this
is an adequate method for most moderately sized greenhouses. Large
specimens are still possible but this is achieved by pruning last year's overwintered plants hard back in spring and either potting them on or top dressing
them.

All *Fuchsia* plants need the tips of shoots pinched back to encourage a
branched compact plant. With those grown as bushes this should start at
the recently potted cutting stage about 8–10 cm (3–4 in) high. Successive
growths' tips should also be removed when they have reached a similar length.
Standard plants, on the other hand, should be encouraged to develop a strong
straight stem. Give these plants small canes as soon as they are potted to
remind you of their future; remove all side shoots that develop, tie the
plant into the cane and replace small canes with larger ones as the plant grows
and is potted. Think how high you want the bottom of the head to be and
allow the plant to keep its side shoots when this height is reached. These
side shoots should be pinched back to get a branched head. When the head is
large enough the main stem can be stopped. At the end of the season the growth
of the head of the standard should be reduced by half. Further pruning to
within one or two buds of the older wood is done in spring as growth is started.
An important point to remember is not to get too enthusiastic about pinching
out the tips. This should stop a good six weeks before you want the plants to
flower to allow the buds to develop at the ends of the shoots. Trailing
varieties should be potted five or six to a hanging basket from 8-cm (3-in) pots.
Continue the pinching out treatment for these as well. I favour a loam-based
compost for all Fuchsias as they need a lot of water during summer and top
heavy plants are much more stable. They also need a lot of feeding in summer
if they are to do well. Vigilance against red spider mite and whitefly is
necessary.

It is interesting to include some species in the collection. *Fuchsia
procumbens* from New Zealand is a small trailing plant which can be grown in
a basket. It has small rounded leaves and curious little orange, purple-blue and
green flowers. These are followed by quite large attractive glaucous pink
berries. *F. fulgens* from Mexico is a large growing strong species best grown as
a bush. Drooping orange-red flowers are produced a little later than most of the
hybrids. This is one of the parents of many of the hybrids.

107

Gardenia   W/T   family *Rubiaceae*

These plants look so lovely when they are offered for sale in shops but never seem to live up to expectations when taken into the greenhouse or home. They do better when kept under tropical conditions but it is feasible to give them a minimum of 13°C (55°F) during winter when they should be kept a bit drier. The foliage is an attractive shiny green but tends to go yellow if not fed enough. They are also lime haters and this should be remembered both with reference to potting compost and to water supply. Sometimes the yellowing of leaves can be attributed to this and a feed of iron sequestrine should work wonders. The plant most commonly sold is *Gardenia jasminioides* from China and Japan. It is grown for its beautifully scented double white flowers which turn a yellowy-cream as they grow older, *G. j. fortuniana* is the most often grown and flowers naturally in summer. The buds need a steady temperature of just above 15°C (60°F) to develop properly. Unfortunately, the flowers are produced sporadically so the plant could never be said to look spectacular. I prefer a similar plant called *Ervatamia divaricata* which is taller and less compact but much easier to grow, not fussy as to compost and freer flowering. This plant flowers on and off throughout the year with scented flowers of a purer white; the only drawback is that one is unlikely to see one outside of botanic gardens.

Gerbera   C   family *Compositae*

Gerbera jamesonii is the Transvaal Daisy from Transvaal and Natal which has become a favourite cut flower in recent years. It is not an easy plant to grow but by no means impossible. Seed should be sown just covered and sharp end down in a light place during March and kept between 18–21°C (65–70°F). Within two to four weeks they should have germinated and the young plants can be grown on, always remembering that they hate being overpotted and loathe being overwatered. Keep them very much on the dry side in a very well-drained loam-based compost and they should flower well. Cool airy conditions are essential; a cold damp unventilated house in autumn and winter will put paid to them quicker than anything. Having established the plants they can be divided and repotted in spring.

Gesneria   W   family *Gesneriaceae*   mostly Brazil

Gesneria cardinalis 'Compacta' (*G. macrantha* 'Compacta', *Rechsteineria cardinalis* 'Compacta' or *Sinningia cardinalis*) is the most commonly grown. It is easily raised from its very fine seed which should be surface sown on to

Chrysanthemum 'Yellow Sands' (an example of a spray chrysanthemum) (right)

Plumbago capensis (below)

Lantana camara
(left)

*Hedychium
gardnerianum*
(below left)

*Passiflora
caeruleo-racemosa*
(below right)

Solandra maxima
(above)

Pavonia multiflora
(right)

Sphaeralcea umbellata
(above left)

Whitfieldia elongata
(above right)

*Rhododendron
brookianum* 'Mandarin'
(left)

moist peat-based compost in spring and kept at between 18–21°C (65–70°F). Prick the seedlings out into a small seed tray and when they are large enough I would pot them three to a 14-cm (5½-in) pot or one to an 8-cm (3-in) pot. As they grow you will notice that they arise from a small tuber. The shoots and leaves are covered with downy hair and the bright red tubular flowers are immensely showy. The plants will flower almost continuously but can be cut back when they become untidy. After a short rest small buds will appear at the surface of the tuber and will grow into a new plant.

Gloxinia   W   family *Gesneriaceae*   South America

The plants we usually call Gloxinias are modern hybrids mostly derived from *Sinningia speciosa*. These are either grown by seed which is very fine and should be surface sown on moist peat-based compost and kept light in a temperature of 21°C (70°F) in February or are acquired as tubers which should be potted with the top of the tuber barely covered with compost from January to March. After flowering during summer the plant will show signs of wanting to die down; gradually reduce watering and store the tuber in its pot in a dry warm place until the following February when it can be repotted and started again. Various methods of propagation are feasible including leaf or stem cuttings and division of the tuber. If you want to grow a real 'over the top' variety from seed try 'Gregor Mendel' which has huge double flowers with bright scarlet petals edged with white. Many more discreet varieties are available in various shades of pink, red and white. Keep water off the leaves as this will scorch them.

Grevillea   C/W   family *Proteaceae*   Australasia

The plant that will spring into most people's minds is the elegant Silk Oak, *Grevillea robusta,* from New South Wales which is widely raised from seed and used as a foliage plant with great effect, especially as a tall plant for greenhouse displays. The leaves are soft and fern-like but I have never seen this plant flower under glass even if grown to 9 m (15 ft) tall. This is by far the easiest to cultivate and does not seem fussy as to soil. I grow mine in a loam-based compost in cool conditions. More difficult to grow are the species that will reward your efforts with curious flowers. *G. banksii* from Queensland is very choice, making a shrub of 2 m (7 ft) tall if planted out. It has silver-grey leaves which are silky beneath and red flowers. Seed will germinate well in late spring at a temperature of 15°C (60°F). They need a lime-free compost and seem to dislike phosphates in the compost. After germination they need looking after very carefully, air circulation being important. Prick them out just as the proper leaves begin to show. Cuttings are possible, if difficult. I have found midsummer as good a time to take them as any; try to take side shoots 10 cm (4 in) long with a heel if possible. They do not like the close atmosphere of a propagating case and are best stood on the greenhouse staging. *G. sulphurea* with its small yellow flowers and *G. rosmarinifolia* with red flowers are good subjects for the cool or frost free house. You will be relieved to know that they are easier to care for and propagate than *G. banksii*.

Griselinia   C   family *Cornaceae*

Griselinia littoralis from New Zealand is too tender to grow outside in most parts of Britain. It does, however, make a useful and attractive evergreen shrub for the greenhouse. It will add height to displays or even make a good specimen in its own right. *G. l.* 'Variegata' is more striking than the plain green species. It will not grow much more than 1.2 m (4 ft) tall when restricted to a pot. Ten-cm (4-in) long cuttings of half ripe shoots root well during summer.

Haemanthus   C/W   family *Amaryllidaceae*   S and Tropical Africa

---

I think this is a splendid group of bulbous plants although they are a little hard to come by. *Haemanthus albiflos*, an evergreen species which forms a good clump of bulbs, is perhaps the most widely grown. It has flowers which by nature of their stamens look like a white paint brush dipped into yellow paint. It is supposed to flower in June but I have found that it will flower at other times. I prefer *H. a.* 'Pubescens' as the leaves are covered with soft hairs. This one flowers in winter. *H. coccineus* is a deciduous species which produces its naked flowers in the late summer or autumn. These also resemble paint brushes, this time dipped into red paint. When these have faded a pair of leaves or sometimes more is produced from each bulb; these are long and beautiful being up to 60 cm (2 ft) long and 20 cm (8 in) wide. These two species are both from South Africa and can grow well in a cool house. However, the only other two species which turn up regularly in cultivation are more demanding and need a warm house. *H. multiflorus* is a deciduous species from tropical Africa. It bears the most spectacular head of bright red flowers in spring. As this fades the leaves are produced on a short maroon spotted stem. *H. katherinae* from Natal is perhaps the showiest of them all. It is almost deciduous but the new growth sometimes begins before the old has completely died down. The flower head is borne at the end of a long stem and is packed with bright red flowers. As the flowers fade red fruits replace them. These contain up to four seeds each of which begins to germinate before the fruit falls off the plant. The flower stem and leaves die down at the end of winter but new shoots will take over and by the end of summer the plant is back in full growth and flower.

I grow all my *Haemanthus* in clay pots and in well-drained loam-based compost with plenty of sharp sand. Plants tend to flower better when slightly potbound so they do not by any means need potting every year unless you are building bulbs up to flowering size. I allow the surface of the soil to dry out between waterings whether they are from South or tropical Africa. Obviously deciduous species will not want more than the occasional watering while resting. It pays not to dry them out completely for a long period as their roots will die off rather than rest. This means that when they are watered properly again they do not have to grow a new root system. Seed can be sown by pressing the ripe berries into seed compost. They should not be covered and kept at 18°C (65°F).

Hardenbergia   C   family *Leguminosae*   Australia and Tasmania

Hardenbergia violacea is a pretty little shrub which in its native habitat would sprawl over mountainsides or scramble up trees. In the greenhouse it needs some support to look well. Little pea-shaped flowers appear from April to June. These are a pinky-purple but there is a white form. It goes under the common name of Sarsaparilla or Australian Lilac. Plants tend to get a little unshapely in which case pruning can be carried out after flowering when cuttings can also be taken. It is prone to attack from red spider mite. Seed should be sown in spring after being soaked for 24 hours and take up to three weeks to germinate.

Hedychium   C/W   family *Zingiberaceae*   India, Himalayas, Malaysia

These are the beautiful sweet smelling Ginger Lilies. *Hedychium gardnerianum* from North India is perhaps the best known. It grows to a height of 2 m (6 ft) planted into the greenhouse border but a little shorter in a pot. Flowers are a showy yellow with bright red stamens. *H. greenei* is a little shorter and the flowers an orange-red. *H. coccineum* has up to 50-cm (20-in) long leaves and red flowers. These plants are almost herbaceous although sometimes their foliage does not completely die down before new shoots emerge from the rhizome. If grown in pots they should be allowed to rest a little during winter although not letting them dry out completely. They are better kept at a minimum of 10°C (50°F) although they can tolerate cool conditions. They should be repotted every other year in spring when division of the rhizomes can also take place. Seeds can be sown in spring after being soaked for two hours and will take three weeks to germinate at 21–24°C (70–75°F).

111

Heliconia   W/T   family *Musaceae*   Tropical America

These plants are closely related to the Banana and are grown for their handsome foilage and the brightly coloured bracts from which the flowers emerge. *Heliconia humilis* has bright scarlet bracts edged with gold. It comes from Trinidad and Brazil and makes a plant of some 1.2 m (4 ft). *H. bihai* is perhaps the most popular and also one of the largest; far too large for a modest greenhouse but it does have superb showy bracts. More sensible is *H. latispatha* whose leaves only reach 1 m (3 ft). This has bracts of orange-red near the base and bright red at the tip. Water these plants well during spring and summer. Throughout the rest of the year they can be kept cooler and drier while they rest. Spring is the time for potting on when division of the rootstock can also take place. Seed may also be sown.

Helxine   C/W   family *Urticaceae*   Corsica

Helxine soleirolii is better known as 'Mind Your Own Business' and I dare say that those gardeners who pull it out of their badly drained gardens as a weed think that others are mad for cultivating it as a greenhouse plant. I think that well-grown plants frothing over the edges of small pots placed as edging plants to the staging are most attractive; especially the silver, variegated and gold forms which are now available. Although plants like moist conditions they will not benefit from overwatering, especially if the water is aimed on top of the mound of foliage in the middle of the pot; it will soon rot and die. A little care taken to water under the foliage will pay dividends. Propagation is very simple. A small tray or pot can be filled with small bunches of foliage pulled carefully away from older plants and inserted as clumps into cutting compost. Once rooted and growing they can be potted separately.

Heptapleurum   W   family *Araliaceae*   SE Asia

Formerly known as *Schefflera, Heptapleurum arboricola* is grown as a foliage plant. Leaves are made up of leaflets that radiate out in a circle giving this plant the name of Parasol Plant. *H. a.* 'Variegata' has yellow spashes on the leaves; *H. a.* 'Geisha Girl' is dark green with rounded leaf tips; *H. a.* 'Hayata' has duller greyish-green leaves with pointed tips. Plants will grow to 2 or 2.5 m (7 or 8 ft) tall. When they are too tall they can be cut back. At the same time the stems can be used as cuttings. Each piece should contain at least two nodes and have the bottom leaf removed. Kept moist and at a minimum of 18°C (65°F) they will take a month to root provided the stem was not too woody.

Hibbertia   C/W   family *Dilleniaceae*

I have grown what I originally thought were two separate species; *Hibbertia volubilis* and *H. scandens*. However, they appear to be identical and *H. scandens* would seem to be the correct name. This is the Guinea Flower of Australia. It is worth growing for its glossy leaves and cheerful yellow flowers that appear sporadically throughout the year. A twiner, this plant will happily reach 4.5 m (15 ft) and keep growing, but thankfully can be cut back freely to the size desired and will flower as small plants. Seed pods will split to reveal red seeds which add to their attraction. Propagation is by cuttings or seed.

Hibiscus   W/t   family *Malvaceae*

These are familiar plants to anybody who has been to warmer countries where they are a very popular garden plant. Those commonly seen abroad are *Hibiscus rosa-sinensis* or varieties of this and are the same as those cultivated in Britain in the greenhouse. There are many different varieties which produce the beautiful showy flowers in many colours and shades of white, pink, red, orange, yellow, cream and purple. *H. r.* 'Cooperi' is grown primarily for its variegated foliage. Whereas the others do well enough in a warm house this makes a much better plant in tropical temperatures. This is also true of *H. schizopetalus* from Kenya and tropical Africa. It has amazing flowers with recurving fringed red petals. It is best grown as a climber and trained up a wall or trellis where it will flower profusely. The only problem with growing *Hibiscus* in pots is that they eventually become leggy and unattractive. Should this happen prune them back hard after most of them have finished flowering in the autumn which will encourage them to grow into better plants. If temperatures have to be lower in winter keep old plants on the dry side and carry out the pruning in spring. This is also a good policy if cuttings are required as they will root better from young material in spring than from old during winter.

In recent years F1 hybrid *Hibiscus* have been developed. *H.* 'Southern Belle' is the one that produces enormous dinner plate sized flowers of 25 cm (10 in) across. However, to get the best of this the seed must be sown early in February and grown on well which means never allowing it to become potbound, feeding and watering well. After flowering the plant can be pruned and kept for a following year. 'Dixie Belle' is another F1 hybrid which does not grow so tall and is an annual. All *Hibiscus* are prone to attack by whitefly.

113

Hippeastrum W family *Amaryllidaceae*

The plants we grow today which come in a wide variety of colour and shade are hybrids that have been crossed and intercrossed over the years. Most growers who have acquired the bulbs ready for potting in winter are unsure about the subsequent resting and growing periods. The important thing to know is that we only allow these plants to die down for our own convenience. They are virtually evergreen and I know a lot of people who keep them growing all year round with spectacular results. Normally one allows the leaves to develop after flowering, giving them plenty of water and food until no more leaves seem to be appearing. Gradually reduce watering until the leaves have died down. This will occur about September time and from now on plants are kept dry and cool. When they are started up again is really up to you; the earliest should be about December in a temperature of 13°C (55°F). However, mostly the plants are started off again in January or February either top dressing them or repotting by planting the bulb back into the pot so that it is half buried. Once the flower spike begins to show it is better to raise the temperature to a minimum of 15°C (60°F). When the flowers open they want to be kept cooler again to make them last longer. If you want a batch of these the cheapest way to achieve this is by sowing seed in spring or when ripe by just covering it and replacing it in a temperature of 15–18°C (60–65°F). When growing young plants on to flowering size they should not be dried off and rested.

Hoya W family *Asclepiadaceae*

These are lovely evergreen climbers with attractive shiny thick leaves. The flowers are waxy and curious in shape and they are frequently referred to as Wax Flowers. There was nothing better than going into the greenhouse at Wisley first thing in the morning and tasting the drop of nectar hanging on the tip of each flower that hung over our heads in the warm corridor. Growing them is extremely easy. They tend to be shallow rooted, especially while establishing, so a light peat-based compost is preferable. The surface of this should be allowed to dry out between waterings. They do not like too hot a temperature and a minimum of 10°C (50°F) during winter is ideal. Most commonly grown is *Hoya carnosa* from Queensland and its varieties which include variegated and coloured leaves. *H. bella* from Burma and Indonesia is a smaller plant which likes to trail rather than climb; ideal for hanging baskets. *H. multiflora* from Malacca is a very upright plant with yellowish flowers and very recurved petals. You will have to search hard to find sources of other species of which there are many. *H. purpureo-fusca* from Java seems to turn up occasionally. Even when not in flower it is easily recognised by the silver blotches on the leaves. Flowers are a maroon-pink colour and I have seen it referred to as *Hoya* 'Silver Pink'. Propagation is straightforward by cuttings in spring. Seed is often produced in long thin pods and can be sown at a temperature of 24°C (75°F). Plants usually flower freely under glass but failure may be due to over feeding; they like to be a little potbound and in good light. Remember never to cut off old flower stalks as more flowers will be produced from them.

Hydrangea C family *Saxifragaceae*

The hardy species *Hydrangea macrophylla* from the Himalayas and China is often used as a pot plant for cool house displays in early summer. This can be done by rooting cuttings in spring and growing them on outside during the summer. They should be allowed just to feel the frost in the autumn which ripens them up before being brought into the cool house where a minimum temperature of 7°C (45°F) is maintained until January, when they are ideally warmed up a little to 13°C (55°F). Larger plants can be grown by bringing the one-year-old plants into flower for a second year. This is much the same procedure except they should be potted after flowering and cut back after they lose their leaves outside in the autumn. Leave either one or two pairs of good buds on the stem and grow them as before. Only the blue flowered varieties need an acid soil as alkaline conditions are apt to turn them pink. Try growing some of the attractive Lacecaps.

Hymenocallis FF/C/W family *Amaryllidaceae* South America

These bulbs are frequently listed in seed catalogues as *Ismene*. They are well worth investing in. Bulbs should be potted between November and January so that the neck of the bulb is just above the surface. The temperature they are grown at can vary between frost free and warm; the warmer they are the earlier they will flower. The flowers are quite spectacular, being shaped rather along the lines of a Daffodil but with the petals (correctly called the perianth tube) divided into curling segments. Most of the flowers are white and highly scented. *Hymenocallis amanceas* from Chile and Peru, *H.* × *festalis* of garden origin and *H.* × *macrostephana* are the ones most usually seen. After flowering, which takes place between April and June, they should be gradually allowed to die down, dried off and stored in a frost free place until the following year. Change the soil every two years otherwise top dressing is adequate.

115

Hypocyrta   W   family *Gesneriaceae*   mostly Brazil

Hypocyrta glabra

Hypocyrta glabra is an excellent little plant which produces neat orange flowers from spring to autumn the strange shape of which gives rise to the name Clog Plant. Even out of flower the small glossy leaves on arching stems are attractive. There are other species, some similar and others large and unruly which are best planted into a hanging basket. In the wild they would trail epiphytically over trees and tree stumps. They like warm humid conditions and a light peaty compost. Cuttings are very easy to root in spring and summer. Keep water off the leaves as regardless of whether they are hairy or not they will be scorched with ugly marks.

Hypoestes   W   family *Acanthaceae*   South Africa

Most people will automatically think of the popular Polka Dot Plant which is *Hypoestes sanguinolenta* grown for the pink dots and splashes on the green leaves which are delightfully furry when young. There is now a form with creamy white dots but I shall always like the pink one best. Occasionally, especially during winter, small purple flowers will be produced and for a while the leaves will be smaller and less showy. Some may say that the flower stems should be cut off but I think they are all part of the character of the plant. After a while a new crop of furry shoots and leaves will appear at the base of the plant. As these grow this is the time to cut down old stems to let the plant regenerate itself. Cuttings can be taken but seed is easily obtained and extremely easy to germinate. There is a lesser known species, *H. aristata* from Natal, which is grown for its flowers which are mauve and white. These are produced in February and are very useful for brightening up the greenhouse. After flowering I would cut the plants back hard but continue to keep warm and water carefully, so that new growth is produced from which 8-cm (3-in) long cuttings can be taken. These can then be grown on. It is necessary to stop these plants at least twice by pinching out the tips to get bushier plants. As they have a long time to wait before flowering they often get too big; striking a later batch of cuttings around June is the answer.

Impatiens   W   family *Balsaminaceae*

Impatiens pseudoviolacea

The sort of 'Busy Lizzie' that everybody used to keep that has pale pink flowers and a rather straggly habit is a species called *Impatiens walleriana* from tropical East Asia. It has two different variegated forms, one with pink flowers and the other orange. There are many hybrids with different coloured flowers including some very pretty doubles and some with flowers like rosebuds. Most of the favourite hybrids are much more compact than the original *I. walleriana*. Many of these are raised by seed annually and used as bedding plants. They can be lifted, cut back and grown in the warm greenhouse during the colder parts of the year. I was never a great fan of *Impatiens* hybrids until the New Guinea hybrids were developed following a plant collecting expedition to that country. These are something special being mostly compact and extremely vibrant with brightly, often colourfully variegated foliage and often huge flowers. They have the advantage of being very easy to propagate and almost as easy as the old 'Busy Lizzie' to grow, perhaps needing just a little bit more warmth. My real favourites will always be the other species, but like all the really interesting greenhouse plants they are difficult to come by. *I. repens* is a trailing plant which surprisingly has bright yellow flowers. A well-grown specimen of this covered in flowers is a cheerful sight. The leaves and stems have a reddish tinge about them. *I. pseudoviolacea* lives up to its name by resembling a violet. It is small growing and produces wonderfully delicate little flowers.

Ipomoea   C/W/T   family *Convolvulaceae*

This name automatically calls to mind the Morning Glory which is the name given to *Ipomoea acuminata*, *I. purpurea* as well as *I. tricolor* (which are sometimes given the generic name of *Convolvulus* or *Pharbitis*). These are easily grown outside during summer but have to be treated as annuals. I would definitely grow *I. acuminata (I. learii)*, the Blue Dawn Flower from tropical America, in the greenhouse. This is an evergreen perennial climbing species which becomes quite woody at the base with age. The flowers are produced in profusion between June and October and are a glorious blue turning pinkish with age. Grown in the warm house it will become a large plant which can be cut down if it becomes tatty or has suffered from red spider mite. It can also be kept in a cool house where it will tend to die down each autumn with the cold but grow back again and flower in the following year. Plants can be pot grown but are best planted out if this is possible. *I. batatas* from the East Indies is the Sweet Potato which does best in tropical conditions. As a straight species it is hardly decorative but if you can get hold of *I. b.* 'Rudolph Rhoers' this is a fine foliage plant with purple leaves. It is best to soak seed for 24 hours before sowing; germination is then usually very good at 18–21°C (65–70°F). Perennial species can be propagated by cuttings and, of course, the Sweet Potato can be propagated by taking small tubers off the main plant at potting time.

Iresine   W   family *Amaranthaceae*   South America

There are two species in cultivation but I find *Iresine lindenii* rather dull and would rather concentrate on *I. herbstii* which is known variously by the rather ghastly names of Beefsteak Plant and Bloodleaf because of its maroon-red leaves and stems, the veins outlined in paler red. *I. h.* 'Brilliantissima' has larger even redder leaves and *I. h. aureo-reticulata* has golden veins on its green leaves. These are easy plants to grow, propagating well from cuttings. It is best to pinch out the shoot tips to encourage bushiness.

Ixora   T   family *Rubiaceae*

These plants only grow well if they have tropical conditions; I have tried them in lower temperatures and their growth almost stands still. If you can give these plants the conditions they like they will live up to their name of 'Flame of the

Woods'. *Ixora coccinea* is the most commonly grown producing heads of many red flowers. It is unusual to find this plant but seed of Ixora mixed hybrids can be bought which are almost certainly hybrids of this East Indian species; red, pink, apricot and white flowered plants can be grown. Seed should be sown just under the surface and kept at a temperature of 21–24°C (70–75°F). You may need patience as germination can take up to four months. I grow the plants in peat-based compost and keep them just a little cooler in winter although never below 15°C (60°F). Any necessary pruning on older plants can be done in spring. Cuttings can be taken at the same time; bottom heat will help these along no end.

Jacaranda   W   family *Bignoniaceae*

Only one species, *Jacaranda mimosifolia* from Brazil, is widely cultivated as a foliage plant. Unfortunately, it has to reach a considerable size before producing its blue flowers. I have never seen a greenhouse specimen flower. However, it has attractive fern-like pinnate leaves produced from a strong straight stem. This makes it useful either as a specimen in its own right or as a background for displays of flowering plants. I would recommend a loam-based compost as, when the plant becomes large, it will need a lot of water and is likely to become dry and unstable at times. Plants will respond well to pruning if one plant is to be kept for a long time; if using them regularly for display I would recommend growing successions of fresh plants from seed. Germination is straightforward and the seed easily obtainable.

Jacobinia   W/T   family *Acanthaceae*   South America

Jacobinia pauciflora

A colourful group of plants, these are easy to grow and flower but need a fair amount of attention by way of cutting back, propagating and spraying. *Jacobinia carnea (J. pohliana* or *J. velutina)* has large heads of pink flowers;

119

J. chrysostephana is often seen for sale and has bright orange flowers; *J. pauciflora* is on a much smaller scale and less upright than the others. Its smaller singly borne flowers are reddish-orange tipped with yellow. *J. suberecta* is another smaller plant which will spread to form a clump if planted into a border. It has downy silver leaves which contrast nicely with the orange-red flowers. As they grow very quickly plants will need renovating regularly. I cut mine hard back to within 2.5 or 5 cm (1 or 2 in) of the base, or if the structure is branching, within a node of older growth. This is best carried out in spring. The resulting new growth can either be grown on or used as cutting material, which roots very quickly. Plants are prone to attack by whitefly.

Jasminum   C/T   family *Oleaceae*

Greenhouse Jasmines are divided as to whether they are almost hardy and will grow in the frost free or cool house or in tropical temperatures. Most, however, are worth growing for their perfume which will pervade the whole atmosphere of the greenhouse. The most easily obtainable is *Jasminum polyanthum* from China which graces British garden centres in great numbers. This is very fragrant and well able to stand cool conditions. The colder the temperature the later its white flowers will be. The bought plants are usually forced; in the cool house flowering is in the spring. It is rampant and if confined to a pot will need pruning after it has flowered, which consists of cutting those long shoots that have just flowered back to within a node of older growth. *J. primulinum (J. mesneyi)* also from China is another nearly hardy plant with bright yellow flowers, also in spring. However, this is not grown for its scent. There should be no problems with either of these. If bought in bud *J. polyanthum* may lose these if it is suddenly placed in a very cool house or subjected to cold draughts. *J. rex* from Thailand and Cambodia is one for the tropical house but unfortunately is scentless. It makes up for this in the beauty of the large white flowers. *J. sambac* from India and *J. nitidum* from the Admiralty Isles are also tropical and both have white scented flowers.

Jatropha   W   family *Euphorbiaceae*   S America

I think one could get away with growing *Jatropha podagrica* in a cool house but it would not do quite so well or be so continuously in flower as if it were grown warm. Known variously as the Gout Plant or Guatemalan Rhubarb this curious succulent from Colombia is a great favourite of mine. For years I only ever saw them in botanical garden collections, then I found one quite by accident in a garden centre. I also discovered that seed is not difficult to come by. It has a swollen stem and usually only about two three-lobed leaves at a time sticking out incongruously from the tip of the stem. Also from this point issue a succession of flowering stems bearing a head of tight red buds which open, one by one, over a long period. By the time one head has finished another has appeared in its place. The golden rule is not to overwater this plant but allow the compost to feel quite dry between watering. Only give it an occasional feed in summer. Plants prefer to be potbound in a deep pot so only pot on when absolutely necessary. If a growing tip can be spared it can be used as a cutting, allowing the cut surface to dry before inserting it into sand. It should be kept much on the dry side. I would not sacrifice the growing tip of my plant even though it would probably branch out with another one. I would rather sow the seed. My own plant produces seed inside a small fruit.

Kaempferia   W   family *Zingiberaceae*   E Tropical Asia

The main problem with this interesting group of plants will be finding them in the first place. They are not at all difficult to grow. In February they should be shaken out of last year's dry soil and potted up into pans of peat-based compost. I do this because the first thing they do is flower. As the flowers appear at the soil surface they would look completely out of scale in a huge pot. Plant several tubers to a pan and water carefully as they grow. To display them I usually place sphagnum moss on the soil surface so that over enthusiastic watering will not blast soil all over them. The flowers are mostly purple and white and very exotic. This treatment applies to the stemless species such as *Kaempferia angustifolia* from the Himalayas and *K. gilberti*. After flowering I pot these up into proper pots as the attractive leaves are long and frequently patterned being mostly dark green above and purple below. By autumn the foliage will die down and plants should remain dry and warm until the following season.

Kennedya   FF/C   family *Leguminosae*   Australia and Tasmania

These climbing plants are easily obtained by seed and are best grown up a pillar or support of some kind. Failing anything else I have found a length of string tied to a stake near the base of the plant and secured above a useful expedient. From a distance they look rather like red flowered runner beans. My favourite is *Kennedya macrophylla* which is very strong and free flowering in summer. *K. rubicunda* flowers a little earlier in late spring. Both these would be worth trying in a frost free house. Plants will respond well to being pruned hard back in order to regenerate old plants which tend to get very old and woody in the centre. A good precaution is to collect seed from the plants regularly.

Kohleria   W   family *Gesneriaceae*

These are attractive hairy-leaved plants which grow from underground running rhizomes. They have a tendency to be straggly and should be staked at a young stage to prevent this. *Kohleria eriantha* from Colombia will bear its red tubular flowers at the top of 60–120-cm (2–4-ft) stems at virtually any time of the year. It is best to keep rooting fresh cuttings 8 cm (3 in) long so as to be able to throw out larger straggly specimens. Alternatively, they can be cut right back after the flowers and fresh new furry growth will soon appear. Propagation can also be by potting up pieces of rhizome in the spring. *K. digitaliflora* should be treated in the same way. It certainly lives up to its name in that the flowers are like foxgloves. The flower tubes are a pinky-purple but the lobes are an amazing canned pea green colour with pink dots. There are various hybrids offered for sale.

Lachenalia   C   family *Liliaceae*   South Africa

There is some confusion with the naming of these attractive little winter and early spring flowering bulbs known as the Cape Cowslips. The most commonly grown used to be known as three different species but are now grouped under *Lachenalia aloides; L. tricolor* is now *L. aloides* and has red yellow and green flowers. Stems and leaves are attractively mottled with purple. *L. aurea* is now *L. a.* 'Aurea' and is tall and golden flowered. *L. nelsonii* is now *L. aloides* 'Nelsonii' whose flowers are orange with a green tinge. Leaves are tinged with purple but not spotted. *L. bulbifera (L. pendula)* is a tall plant with stunning bright coral-red flowers tipped with purple. One occasionally finds other species but these are the main ones offered for sale. Bulbs should be potted up in August or September, several to a pot, and covered with 2.5 cm (1 in) of the well-drained loam-compost they favour. Having watered them in well the pots should be stood in the cool house and only watered again when the surface of the soil is well dried out. More water can be given as the plants grow. After flowering water can be gradually withheld until the leaves turn yellow and die down. They should then be kept dry until potting time. It does them no harm to be grown a little warmer (13°C, 55°F) but they are liable to become floppy and in need of support.

Lagenaria   T   family *Cucurbitaceae*   Asia and Tropical Africa

Lagenaria vulgaris (L. siceraria) is the Bottle Gourd or Calabash Cucumber grown for its variously shaped fruits which are not edible but put to a variety of other uses. This is great fun to grow but, although plants will do quite well grown outdoors as annuals, the fruits rarely have a long enough season to mature properly. If you have the room in a greenhouse a good harvest of gourds should be possible. Specimens are best grown in borders but will still do well in large pots. Seed should be sown in February to give the longest season possible but temperatures of 21–24°C (70–75°F) are optimum and will have germination starting in three days. If at least warm conditions are not available initially it is better to delay sowing until April or May. Thereafter the higher the temperature the bigger and harder skinned the gourds will be. Good results can still be had with a minimum of 10°C (50°F). Pinch the tips of the plants out when they reach 1.5 m (5 ft) and train subsequent lateral shoots along horizontal wires. Watch for flower production and if they are female flowers (those with a miniature fruit waiting behind the flower) pollinate these by hand and stop the end of the shoot at the second leaf after the flower. Should the fruit fail to develop then cut the whole lateral back to the first leaf joint. Another lateral will grow and you can try again. In this way; with one fruit per lateral and two leaves beyond it you are controlling the mass of leafy growth that would otherwise have formed and limiting the number of gourds so that they will grow large. When you are satisfied that you have plenty of gourds simply prevent further growth and let what you have mature nicely. It is not easy to find other plants compatible with the gourd so it may well be a case of turfing other plants outside for the summer and sticking to gourds and cucumbers.

Lagerstroemia FF/C family *Lythraceae*

Lagerstroemia indica is the Crepe Myrtle from China and makes a very attractive late summer flowering shrub which can be almost hardy outside. Do not be dismayed if your plant drops all its leaves after flowering because they are deciduous. Plants are best pruned quite hard in winter to retain a compact shape. Cuttings can be taken in spring choosing short shoots with a heel. It is possible to train straight specimens as standards by taking off all the side shoots until the head is to be developed. The flowers are various shades of pink. There is also a white form.

Lantana W family *Verbenaceae*

Lantana camara from Jamaica and its varieties are the plants most likely to be seen and are very useful shrubs which will rarely be out of flower. The flower heads have fascinated many people by frequently containing flowers of two different colours; the species is pink and yellow but all sorts of forms and cultivars, involving also red, orange and white, occur. At some stage, usually in February, flowers will have to be sacrificed in order to prune the plant as they

123

will become straggly and tired looking after a while. Cut the stems back to within 10–15 cm (4–6 in) of the base or of older stems. The leaves and stems are prickly and have a rather unpleasant smell. I think the common name of Yellow Sage is being rather unkind to the herb. Visitors from South Africa are amazed when they see us carefully cultivating it as not only does it grow as a weed in their country but they can be prosecuted for allowing it to grow on their land, since it is poisonous to cattle. The only point that would make me dubious about growing it is its attraction to whitefly. Any plant I have ever owned has never seemed to be clean of these despite my efforts to control them. *L. selloviana* from Montevideo is a useful greenhouse groundcover plant with pinkish-purple flowers. Cuttings of these are best taken in spring and root very easily. Seed, usually of mixed hybrids, is easily obtained and should be soaked for one hour in hand hot water prior to sowing.

Lapageria FF/C family *Liliaceae* Chile

You will soon find out that *Lapageria rosea,* the Chilean Bell Flower, dislikes lime if you unknowingly pot it into ordinary compost; growth begins to turn brown and new shoots shrivel. A quick move into a lime-free mixture will soon set it right. These wonderful plants, with long-lasting waxy bell-shaped flowers produced almost all year round, can be grown in pots but are much better in a bed with a trellis for them to climb. They like cool shaded conditions during summer and must never be allowed to dry out at the roots. The species has deep pink flowers and there is a white form. Hybrids between the pink and white give us a choice of pale pink, creamy-white, salmon, bicolours and doubles. Propagation by cuttings is a slow process but not impossible. I have found they are more likely to root outside a propagating case than in it; the main problem is finding good shoot material to make the cuttings from. Semi ripe stems in June are preferable. Plants can also be layered, pegging shoots down into pots or trays of compost. The time to sow seed is whenever they are ripe, squeezing them straight from the pod on to the compost and covering them lightly. Any delay will reduce the chance of germination which will be very good if they are fresh and best at temperatures of 15–18°C (60–65°F). The worst pests are aphids which attack fresh young growth. Fortunately, these are easily controlled although take care as some chemicals will damage young shoots. Mealy bug can be a problem.

Ledebouria C family *Liliaceae*

It is very hard to find either *Ledebouria violacea (L. hyacintha),* sometimes called *Scilla socialis* 'Violacea', or any reference to it although it is widely grown by gardeners and passed around from collection to collection. It is a compact plant from India with attractively spotted leaves and greenish-violet tubular flowers in June. Being bulbous one would assume that they would have to be kept on the dry side; although this is safest during the coldest weather they can survive being almost waterlogged in summer and are good tough little plants to grow, quickly filling a pot with bulbs. Potting and division can take place in spring.

Leea   T   family *Vitaceae*

I do not think that *Leea coccinea* from Burma is a wildly exciting plant but it has appeared as a 'regular' in garden centres in recent years. It is grown basically for its rather handsome foliage but does little better than struggle unless given a tropical temperature. When about 30 cm (1 ft) tall a head of small dark red flowers will be produced but they are hardly showy. Propagation is by seed sown in spring.

Leptospermum   FF/C   family *Myrtaceae*   Australasia

Perhaps a lot of people have bought these splendid shrubs in flower from a garden centre and been disappointed when they died during their first winter. In most areas they definitely need greenhouse protection, but given this will reward your efforts by being covered with little flowers in late spring. *Leptospermum scoparium* from New Zealand is the most popular. Although it has white flowers it is usually the varieties which are sold; 'Red Damask' is a double deep red, 'Keatleyi' is pink, 'Nicholsii' is red with purplish-bronze foliage; pale pink and double whites are also seen. Plants will flower well in pots but planted out will grow into tall shrubs which have fine attractive foliage when not in flower. *L. citratum* is particularly nice, not just for its white flowers but for the lemon scented foliage. Try raising some from seed. If you have enough plants some can be planted outside in a sheltered spot. If this experiment fails there will always be reserve plants in the greenhouse. Cuttings can be taken after flowering and rooted at 15°C (60°F).

Liriope   FF/C   family *Liliaceae*   Japan, China

Liriope platyphylla (L. muscari) is reliably hardy outside but its evergreen grass-like leaves become so tatty after the ravages of winter weather that it is never as attractive as it should be. This is a very good reason for growing this and the even more attractive *L. p.* 'Variegata', which has creamy-yellow stripes

125

running the length of the leaf, under glass. The leaves will form a good clump either in pots or planted into a border. During later summer and autumn flower spikes of dark purple flowers are produced, which resemble the flowers of Grape Hyacinth the generic name for which is *Muscari*. Blue-black berries follow the flowers. *L. p.* 'Grandiflora' has lavender flowers and *L. p.* 'Monroe White' is self explanatory. They prefer a well-drained loam compost and can be divided and repotted in spring.

Lonicera   C   family *Caprifoliaceae*

Lonicera hildebrandiana is one of the only two tender honeysuckles usually found in greenhouse collections both of which are evergreen and flower in summer. This is the Giant Honeysuckle from Burma, Siam and China. It is a plant on a rather large scale and needs a fair amount of head room to do it justice. Each flower is up to 15 cm (6 in) long and, as they begin white and fade to orange, it gives the appearance of having flowers of different colours on the same plant. They are only faintly scented. *L. sempervirens* from southern USA is the Trumpet Honeysuckle and has unscented flowers which are red outside and orange-yellow inside the tube. Propagation is by 8–10-cm (3–4-in) long cuttings taken in July or August and rooted at 15°C (60°F).

Lotus   C   family *Leguminosae*

Lotus berthelotii from Tenerife is rightly named the Coral Gem. It is a perennial with long trailing branches covered with silvery needle-like leaves which make an excellent foil for the scarlet claw-shaped flowers which appear in May. This is an excellent plant for a hanging basket but is not easy to grow. It will thrive in cool airy conditions but dislikes being overwatered to a point where it almost pays to let plants nearly begin to droop before daring to water them again. Cuttings taken in spring should be grown on and planted into baskets for flowering the following year.

Luculia   C/W   family *Rubiaceae*   E Asia

Luculia gratissima from the Himalayas becomes quite a large shrub bearing heads of pale pink beautifully scented flowers during autumn and winter. They can be grown in pots but will make better plants if planted out. The important thing is to give them lots of water and food during summer when they are building up to flower. When the flowers have faded it is good policy to prune

126

plants back hard otherwise they become too tall, straggly and in need of support. After pruning they should be kept very much on the dry side until spring and good growing conditions return. Cuttings rooted with bottom heat in summer are usually successful. It is worth sowing seed but be prepared for up to three years of growing plants on before flowering size is reached; the wait is worth while. There is a summer flowering species; *L. grandiflora* from Bhutan which has very long leaves and large fragrant tubular white flowers. As, of course, with many other plants, they will benefit greatly from being well fed and watered during summer.

Luffa W/T family *Cucurbitaceae*

I wonder how many people thought, as I did for years, that Loofah Sponges used all over the world as bath time back scrubbers came from the sea. There are of course sea sponges but the Loofah is the inner structure of the fruit of *Luffa cylindrica* which is related to the cucumber. Most of the best sponges are grown and processed in Japan by immersing the ripe fruits in tanks of running water until the outer wall disintegrates. To grow plants that will produce good sponges we really need to give this plant tropical conditions, as the fruits which resemble plump cucumbers need to ripen from green to brown before the flesh will come away easily from the inner structure. Seed should be sown at the beginning of March and culture should be as for *Lagenaria* (see page 122).

Maurandia C family *Scrophulariaceae* Mexico

These make attractive climbers for the cool or frost free house which although best treated as annuals can be pruned back after flowering and grown again. Seed should be sown early in spring at 15°C (60°F) to flower well in the first year. *Maurandia barclaiana* from Mexico has triangular leaves and rose-purple flowers produced during a long period between spring and autumn. *M. erubescens* has triangular downy leaves and large rosy-pink hairy flowers with a white tube produced during summer and autumn. *M. scandens* has smaller flowers that can vary in colour from pale mauve to a luxurious red. Whether grown in pots or planted out they will need the support of strings or wire for their vigorous climbing shoots. As an alternative to seed, cuttings can be taken from short side shoots.

Medinilla   T   family *Melastomataceae*

You will be very lucky to find any other species than *Medinilla magnifica* offered for sale but this is such a splendid plant that we should not be too downcast. It does need tropical conditions although it will survive lower temperatures during very short rest periods immediately after flowering when it can be kept drier. This plant from the Philippines will flower several times during the year; usually in May and June and again in the autumn or winter. The common name of Rose Grape is most descriptive as this is what the pinkish-purple flowers resemble, hanging down in a spectacular large bunch as they do. As a result these plants need to be displayed in a high place when in flower so that admirers can appreciate the full beauty of the flowers from below. When not in flower the large rounded leaves are attractive in themselves. Cuttings are of half ripe wood when you can bear to spare it. Plants are slow growing and will not need potting very often. The more warm, humid and well fed they are kept the more flowers they will produce.

Metrosideros   C   family *Myrtaceae*

A little bit unusual but often seen for sale as plants or seed is *Metrosideros tomentosa,* the New Zealand Christmas Tree. This, although it reaches a large tree in its native New Zealand, will produce its summer flowers as a fairly small plant in a pot. It is not so much the petals of the flowers that are attractive but the long crimson stamens giving them a bottle brush appearance. Cuttings can be taken after flowering.

Mimosa   T   family *Leguminosae*   Tropical America

For those who think I am about to launch into a description of florists' 'mimosa' then please turn to *Acacia. Mimosa pudica* is the Sensitive Plant grown for the amusement of touching the leaves and seeing them close up and the stems bow down to the ground; perhaps also for the pretty round pink flower heads produced towards the end of summer. High temperatures are not required for germinating the seed. I have germinated a batch in July without any artificial heat at all. However, to get better plants it is best to sow them early in the year at 18–21°C (65–70°F). Plants should be grown on as warm and humid as possible so that by the end of summer large flowering plants can be had. I plant three small plants to a pot in peat-based compost to produce a good potful.

They are usually treated as annuals but can be pruned hard almost to the base after which they will sprout again, but they never make as good a plant. These are great favourites with children.

Mirabilis   FF/C/W   family *Nyctaginaceae*

Mirabilis jalapa is the Marvel of Peru and is a pretty little plant that can be grown outside in summer but is much better under glass away from the ravages of rain and wind. Plants can arrive as long tuberous roots which are potted in spring and watered carefully into growth, or as seed sown thinly and evenly in spring at 18°C (65°F) when they will germinate in two to three weeks. Plants are only 60 cm (2 ft) in height and produce trumpet-shaped flowers throughout the summer that can be white, yellow or bright pink. These flowers are closed in the morning and open during the afternoon so that their name is Four o'Clock. They will die down in the autumn and should be taken from their pots and stored in a dry frost free place in a box of peat or sand much like a *Dahlia* tuber.

Monstera   T   family *Araceae*   W Indies, Tropical America

Splendid foliage plants; *Monstera deliciosa,* the most well known, is the Swiss Cheese Plant from Mexico. Tropical temperatures are necessary for these to grow well and produce really huge glossy green leaves with indentations and holes. It is not really feasible to grow them in a small greenhouse but in a large humid tropical house they will grow much as they do in the wild; climbing up pillars and easily attaining heights of 4.5 m (15 ft) or more. Aerial roots will grow in profusion and hang down, often rooting into the greenhouse floor. These roots are produced in the wild to help the plants climb up the trees. The roots cling to the bark of trees and search out moisture and leafy compost caught in niches high up in the branches. Occasionally they are a nuisance when they invade other plants and some can be cut off without doing any harm to the plant, especially if it has a good root system inside its pot. Propagation is by taking sections of stem each containing two leaves. Cut above the top one and below the bottom one which is then cut off. The cutting should be inserted into a pot of cutting compost and left to root in a warm humid place. Plants will occasionally produce flowers and edible fruits which have a pineapple flavour. Seed is best germinated at a high temperature, 24–26°C (75–80°F).

129

Musa FF/C/W/T *Musaceae*

Fortunately the popularity of Banana plants has meant that they are not difficult to find and an impressive range of seed can be chosen from. For a frost free house *Musa basjoo* from Japan is suitable. *M. ensete,* the Abyssinian Banana, will do well in a cool house and for a small warm house *M. coccinea* from China will only grow to 1.2 m (4 ft) when it will produce very ornamental yellow flowers with bright red bracts tipped with yellow. Also growing to 1.2 m (4 ft) is *M. velutina,* which bears ornamental bright pink fruits after its orange-yellow flowers. For a fruiting banana choose *M. cavendishii* sometimes called *M.* × *paradisiaca* 'Dwarf Cavendish' as this is the smallest of the fruiters. However, it will need rich soil, humidity and a temperature of 18°C (65°F) to fruit well. After fruiting the main part of the plant dies and leaves one or more suckers to grow in its place. Banana seeds are large and hard. They will benefit from being soaked for two days before sowing and should have a temperature of 18–21°C (65–70°F) to germinate which will take as little as one month in late spring or summer. I prefer to grow bananas in tubs or large pots so that they can be moved to give each other more space. I prefer a loam-based compost for plants growing cool and peat-based for those in tropical heat and humidity.

Mutisia FF/C family *Compositae* S America

Mutisia ilicifolia is a climber with holly-like leaves which end in a long tendril. The flowers are pinky-mauve and 5–8 cm (2–3 in) across. They are produced almost continuously making this an extremely useful plant for brightening up the greenhouse. Cuttings of half ripe shoots can be taken in spring. Plants are sometimes available as seed although that gathered in Britain is never very reliable.

Nerium C/W family *Apocynaceae*

Nerium oleander from Mediterranean regions, usually referred to simply as Oleander, is a very reliable and showy flower for the greenhouse, which if grown in tubs or pots can also be moved on to the patio during hot dry weather in summer; I would put it back inside during times of wind and rain as these will spoil the flowers. As there are different forms with different coloured flowers quite a collection of dark and pale pink, white, creamy-yellow, doubles and a variegated form with lovely creamy stripes on the leaf can be grown. I give my plants plenty of water and liquid feed during spring and early summer while they are building themselves up to flower from about June onwards. After flowering they can be pruned back. Cuttings are easily rooted from shoots taken any time during spring and summer. Seed can also be sown. Be careful with the plant as all parts of it are poisonous. Unfortunately, though, they are not poisonous to mealy bug which will make a meal of them if not controlled.

Nymphaea   W/T   family *Nymphaeaceae*

Very few people think of landscaping their greenhouse or conservatory but this is perfectly feasible, and water can be included which opens up the possibility of growing temperate and tropical waterlilies. The culture of these is very similar to growing them in outdoor ponds; they should be potted into rich loamy soil with a layer of gravel below and on the top to prevent the soil from floating away. This should be done in spring and the pots sat in the water so that to begin with they are only just covered. As they grow, which ideally requires a temperature of 18–21°C (65–70°F), they can be gradually lowered so that the fully grown leaves float on the surface. If you cannot raise the temperature sufficiently wait until the natural temperature is higher. For the winter when they are dormant one is supposed either to drain the water off or lift the tubers and store them in damp sand. I have always got away with simply leaving them in the water at a minimum of 10°C (50;°F) with good results. *N. capensis* is the Cape Blue Water Lily from South Africa. Flowers are a glorious blue and stand 13 cm (5 in) above the water. *N. stellata* the Blue Lotus is lavender-blue with a golden centre. There are several hybrids; *N.* × 'St Louis' is a lovely lemon colour. Propagation is by dividing the tuber at potting time. Pot up small pieces and when new plants have been formed remove these from the old piece of tuber and grow on. Some of them produce small plantlets around the leaf stalk which can be pulled off and potted up. Seed can be sown in pans of compost just covered by water at 21°C (70°F).

Ochna   W   family *Ochnaceae*

Only one species, *Ochna serrulata,* is easily obtainable. It comes from Natal and makes a medium sized shrubby plant which has attractive red tints to the new growth. The flowers are yellow and appear in spring but more attractive

Ochna serrulata

by far are the fruits which follow. These are shiny black and sit on a waxy calyx which recurves from them and is bright red. Very little pruning is required. Cuttings may be taken in summer or seed sown in spring.

Odontonema   W/T   family *Acanthaceae*   Tropical America

These plants really need tropical temperatures to do well but can be grown adequately in a warm house. The winter flowers of *Odontonema schomburgkianum* from Colombia always come as a shock to me; going by the appearance of the plant I always expect an upright spike of bracts and flowers much like *Pachystachys* to which it is related. Instead, the flower spike drapes elegantly down the plant and the red tubular flowers hang from it. Plants grow very well from cuttings and I like to plant three young plants to an 18-cm (7-in) pot of peat-based compost to give a good display. After flowering plants should be cut down almost to the base and either the resulting new shoots can be grown on to flowering size or they can be taken as cuttings.

Oplismenus   W   family *Graminae*

The most commonly grown is *Oplismenus hirtellus* 'Variegatus' which has leaves variegated with white and pink. At first glance one could be forgiven for thinking that it was a *Tradescantia* as this is what it resembles, trailing over the sides of the pot and making a most attractive edging plant for displays on the greenhouse staging. However, it gives itself away as being a grass when it produces its dark red flowers at the ends of the shoots in summer. It can be propagated in much the same way as *Tradescantia* by taking short nodal cuttings of shoot tips. An excellent hanging basket plant.

Orchids

The growing of these exotic plants can often become an obsession. Some growers manage to include one or two amongst a collection of other plants and are quite satisfied. Others find the whole group totally absorbing and concentrate on collecting and flowering them alone.

The most important thing to understand is that most orchids are epiphytic and would grow on the branches and trunks of trees. They do not absorb any nourishment from the tree but merely use them as supports. It is lovely if you can rig up a series of dead tree branches for your orchids to grow on. If you have not got the space then small pieces of cork oak bark can be bought for the same purpose. Orchids can be easily attached either on their own or with a pad of Osmunda fibre or sphagnum moss to help them anchor to the branch. Larger orchids can be held by staples and smaller ones by binding of nylon fishing line. Watering of these consists of thoroughly wetting the roots using a hose pipe with a fine nozzle lance attached. Obviously the amount of water given will vary according to weather, temperature and whether the plants are in their resting stage. Watering is different to damping down which is much lighter and done to increase humidity. If you are going to have orchids growing epiphytically there must be somebody on hand to damp down, often four times per day if it is hot and sunny. Alternatively, an automatic misting system must be installed. Given a few years for these orchids to establish you will be rewarded by a fascinating and unusual display.

Even terrestrial orchids would grow in a very light soil of leaf litter. If you are going to grow orchids in pots they must have a special orchid compost which usually consists of orchid grade bark: 4 parts, perlite: 1 part and charcoal: 1 part. This may sound like a peculiar compost but the last thing an orchid wants is for its roots to be surrounded by wet fine compost. After a time the special bark mix will begin to break down into smaller pieces and when this happens the orchid should be repotted.

Even when there is sufficient water in the compost the surface of the bark invariably feels dry to the touch so this cannot be used as an indicator. The best way to test whether you should water or not is to feel the weight of the pot. If it flies up in the air water is obviously required, however if you can feel a weight in the pot there will be sufficient water inside. The ideal staging is slats of wood over a gravel tray. In this way water drains right away from the bottom of the pot but the plants get the benefit of humidity rising from water in the gravel.

Orchid compost usually contains no fertiliser. Liquid feeding is thus of great importance and I would recommend using a special orchid liquid feed which usually has foliar feeding properties as well. This is essential particularly for orchids growing on trees or cork bark. During the growing season feed should only be applied weekly but every fourth week miss out the feed and rinse the compost through with pure water as this will prevent the build up of salts in the compost which could be harmful to the plants. Some orchids benefit from high potash feeds when they are building themselves up to flower.

Much thought must be given to shading as plants will begin to yellow and produce scorched patches on the leaves if over exposed to light. However, good winter light is necessary for most of them.

If something goes wrong with an orchid it can die a lot quicker than an ordinary plant. Check them over regularly and if there are signs of overwatering, i.e. yellowing and drooping leaves, a spongy feel to the base of the plant and very wet compost, carefully take the plant out of its pot, get rid of all the old stagnant compost and repot it into some new dry mix. Leave for one day before watering in. Thereafter ensure that the pot is very light before watering again. Keep a close look out for red spider mite on thin leaved orchids and for mealy bug, scale and aphids on the rest. Sometimes slugs and even cockroaches can be pests in large collections and are a particular nuisance for eating flower buds just as they are developing.

The orchids you choose to grow will be determined mainly by the minimum winter temperature you can maintain.

Cool House Orchids

Cymbidium The only drawback with these winter flowering orchids is their size. They are a graceful plant even when not in flower but if your aim is to grow the largest number of orchids as possible you will not fit many of these into an average sized greenhouse. Do not be tempted to pack them in otherwise their health will suffer. *Cymbidium* are naturally epiphytic and the species originate from the foothills of the Himalayas down to Burma. Many people have trouble getting them to flower. Providing they are healthy and in good light this is most probably due to temperature. A night temperature of 10°C (50°F) is ideal with a rise of 4–5°C (8–10°F) during the day. If it is not possible to maintain that rise during the day then the best policy is to drop the night temperature accordingly. These orchids flower better if they are given space and plenty of ventilation when temperatures allow. I stand mine outside the greenhouse in a semi shaded place in summer. Keep the plants drier in August and September which encourages flower spike development. As soon as spikes have formed they can be given more water. Potting, if needed, should be done after flowering although they will flower better if undisturbed. Whilst potting plants they can be divided. Each pseudobulb or swelling with leaves growing from it should have two or three green leafless 'backbulbs' attached to it.

Masdevallia These epiphytic orchids come from Central and Southern

Masdevallia kimballiana

America. I really like them but they are possibly not as showy as some other orchids as it is their sepals which provide the attraction rather than the petals. They do not have pseudobulbs and, as such, should not be allowed to dry out too much between waterings. *M. kimballiana* is an attractive burnt orange.

Bletilla B. striata is a terrestrial orchid almost hardy enough to be grown outside but is well worth planting in a pot. A compost of equal parts of loam, peat, grit, leaf mould and sphagnum moss is more suitable than bark. Pink flowers appear in May. The plants will go dormant during winter but should not be dried right out.

Warm House
Odontoglossum Naturally, these plants grow at high altitudes and although modern hybrids are more adapted to doing well in 'captivity' as it were, it still pays to keep a good circulation of air and give ample shading in summer to keep temperatures down. These are epiphytic orchids which bear quite spectacular flowers often from very small plants which gives the collector the chance to accommodate a good selection.

Paphiopedilum These are sometimes still referred to as *Cypripedium*. I dislike intensely the huge hybrid flowers which seem fat and bloated to me. I much prefer the species and daintier hybrids and find straightforward *P. insigne* which must be the commonest of the lot very attractive. *P. hirsutissimum* is a very distinct species from Assam with twisted spotted purply petals and dark hairs all over the flowers and stems. *P. bracteatum* has a delicate shape. These are terrestrial orchids and can be divided culturally into green leaved types

135

Phaphiopedilum bracteatum

which are cooler growing and mottled leaved types which need a warmer more moist atmosphere. The former will grow and flower happily with a minimum temperature of 13°C (55°F) but the latter prefer a minimum of 15°C (60°F). Shading for both must be closely attended to. Keeping moisture away from the centre of the plants, where they may easily rot, is essential.

Dendrobium These are one of my favourite groups of orchid. They are epiphytes which grow naturally from India down through eastern Asiatic countries to Australia. It is important when growing them to know whether you are dealing with an evergreen or deciduous type. Evergreens hang on to their thicker tougher leaves for several years whereas the deciduous will lose theirs every year in the dry period before flowering. Watch the growth of these deciduous ones carefully as during autumn they will produce a pair of terminal leaves with no little shoot in between. This is their signal that they are ready to rest. Give only enough water every month or so to prevent absolute shrivelling until the flower buds appear. If too much water is given during this resting period they will not produce many flowers but small plantlets instead which can be taken off and grown on separately.

Pachystachys   W/T   family *Acanthaceae*   South America

This is represented in cultivation by the lesser known *Pachystachys coccinea* and *P. lutea* which has become much more widely available in recent years. *P. coccinea* is more demanding in that it prefers a more tropical temperature. It makes a tall plant of 1.2 m (4 ft) before producing its large heads of green bracts and bright red flowers. *P. lutea* from Peru lives up to its name of Lollipop Plant by freely producing long-lasting heads of bright yellow bracts and white tubular flowers almost continuously throughout the year. During winter, flower production tends to tail off and the plants can be rested for a

Pachystachys lutea

while before being pruned hard back in the spring. The shoots produced can either be grown on to make a new plant, in which case repotting or top dressing will be necessary, or they can be used as cuttings to raise a new batch.

Palms

One is more likely to grow these graceful plants in a conservatory than a greenhouse as they tend to be on the large side and are very much a decorative plant to form a backdrop for other plants in a display.

They are easy to grow but are prone to becoming dry at the tips of their leaves. This is caused by dry air. If a conservatory is to be a room for plants as well as for people it is essential to think about how decorations and furniture can be tied in with the need to keep the air humid by damping down or spraying. There must also be adequate provision for shade if leaves are not to be scorched. Another scourge of palms is red spider mite which are encouraged by dry air. A constant vigil must be maintained to spot and treat this pest before the palms are ruined. Remember that spraying under the leaves regularly will discourage them. In the wild, palms grow very large and the specimens we grow are only juvenile forms which are much more tender than the palms we might see along the Mediterranean coast in full sun.

Some palms such as *Chamaerops, Livistonia, Phoenix* and *Trachycarpus* can tolerate cool conditions. Apart from *Phoenix* these are also all palms that have fan shaped leaves. The other palms need warm temperatures to do well. I prefer to pot them into a loam-based compost because as they are large plants and will need a lot of water peat-based mixes will become drier, lighter and easier to knock over. Watering palms is a case of allowing the surface to become dry between waterings but not for longer than a day.

Choosing Palms

Trachycarpus is able to grow outside in the milder parts of Britain so I would give this one a miss for the conservatory. *Washingtonia, Livistonia* and *Phoenix* are very majestic but grow easily as wide as they are high and have quite stiff leaves. They are probably the most tolerant of dry air and bright light. They will certainly lend a Mediterranean air to the area they inhabit. For a soft palm that is more upward growing, graceful and elegant *Howea belmoreana* which used to be called *Kentia* is the best choice. These will reach a good 2.5 m (8 ft) tall and need to be warmer, more humid and slightly shaded in summer. For a smaller palm I would recommend *Chamaedorea elegans* which used to be *Neanthe* and is widely referred to as the Parlour Palm. This has a nasty habit of turning yellow if in full sun during summer or not fed sufficiently. There will come a time when they have outgrown their attractiveness. Palms cannot be pruned as they will not shoot from places lower down on the stem. *Rhapis excelsa* is a super little bushy palm from Japan. *R. e.* 'Variegata' looks great potted into a Japanese style glazed pot. Although able to do well in a cool house it will do equally well in warm or even tropical conditions.

If you have a warm or tropical house you will be able to grow one of my favourites which is *Caryota mitis* the Fish Tail Palm from Burma and Malaya. The leaflets really do resemble the tattered edges of a fish's tail in a most unusual and attractive way. Offsets are produced around the base of the plant. This is quite common with palms and when they have grown about three leaves with hopefully a few roots of their own they can be detached and grown on. Do not be dismayed by heights of 4.5–7.5 m (15–25 ft) being quoted in books as this is only reached very slowly and only usually in the wild. Before yours gets anywhere near that you should have some offsets to provide newer, more sensibly sized, plants.

I know they look really nice but I would avoid buying one of those palms growing out of a coconut on the surface of the compost. There have been a lot offered for sale in recent years and I have not seen one which was not infected with red spider mite. For some reason they seem to love them more than any other palm. Even a clean looking plant from a good garden centre may be harbouring eggs which will hatch out and infect all your other plants.

It is possible to germinate palms from seed but it can be a painfully slow process. Soak the seed for at least two hours in warm water before sowing. Use a peat-based seed compost and place the pot in the dark at 24°C (75°F) to germinate. Keep this moist and occasionally dig into the soil to see if a root has been produced. If it has it is best to pot on to a deeper pot so that there is room for this root to grow. A shoot will follow shortly.

Pandanus   T   family *Pandanaceae*

Pandanus veitchii from Polynesia is the Screw Pine or Pandan. It is a good
foliage plant while it remains small but, even when restricted to a small pot,
these plants can grow into monsters. Pushing past a *Pandanus* is no joke as the
90-cm (3-ft) long white and yellow striped leaves have a lethally sharp toothed
edge. They also have the habit of producing low aerial prop roots which tend
to force plants out of their pots, making repotting necessary and difficult every
two to three years. Fortunately, there is *P. v.* 'Compacta' with smaller leaves
up to 60 cm (2 ft) long.

Propagation can be by seed, suckers or offsets that are produced around large
plants. To handle plants at potting and offset detaching time it is best to wrap
the leaves in newspaper or hessian. They really do need tropical conditions to
grow well and are almost too easy to grow. Not a plant for a small greenhouse
but a very majestic specimen for a large tropical display house.

Pandorea   C/W   family *Bignoniaceae*   Australia

I was not going to include these attractive climbing plants initially as I did not
think they were available. However, it is possible to buy seed. *Pandorea
jasminioides,* the Bower Plant, has attractive shiny foliage and trumpet-shaped
pink flowers with darker pink centres in summer. *P. pandorana (P. australis)*
which goes under the name of Wonga Wonga Vine has quite finely cut foliage
and smaller yellow or pale pink flowers with violet spotted throats. They can
be grown in pots provided they are given some support but do better when
planted out, reaching up to 3 m (10 ft) or more if left unpruned. If the
greenhouse has a sunnier side they should be planted in this. Attention to
watering and feeding during spring and summer will pay dividends in flower
production. Cuttings of half ripe wood can be taken in summer. There is a very
similar genus in the same family called *Podranea* which interestingly enough
is an anagram of *Pandorea*.

Passiflora   FF/C/W/T   family *Passifloraceae*   South America

The central column of the flower represents the scourging post, the three
stigmas the three nails, the five stamens the five wounds, the corona filaments
the crown of thorns, the calyx the halo of glory and the ten petals the apostles
minus Judas and Peter. This is how the early missionaries in South America
compared the various parts of the Passion Flower to Christ's Passion and how
this exotic group of climbers acquired their strange name.

139

Passiflora × allardii

The most commonly grown is *Passiflora caerulea* which is hardy in some parts of Britain, producing its white flowers with mauve-blue filaments between June and September. However, this is also an excellent specimen for the frost free house. Fruits are often borne which are ornamental rather than edible. A more unusual choice for the frost free or cool house is *P. herbertiana* from Australia with three-lobed leaves and small orange-green flowers in late summer. If you want to grow passion fruits to eat, then *P. edulis,* the Purple Granadilla, whose wrinkly brown fruits are often seen for sale in supermarkets, is a good one to try. This likes warm conditions and should produce fruit in its second year from seed. Incidentally they do not have to become wrinkled before they are fit to eat; a purplish-yellow colour and slight toughening of the skin is a sure sign that they are ripe. It will need a fair bit of head room to fruit well. Flowers are white and purple; interesting but not the showiest. Fruit of *P. ligularis,* the Sweet Granadilla, which also likes warm conditions is in my opinion the best flavour; this is an even larger plant from Peru with big heart-shaped leaves. The fruit is quite large and is ripe when yellow. *P. quadrangularis* the Giant Granadilla has an extremely showy flower and edible fruits but prefers a more tropical temperature. *P. mollissima* for the warm house has beautiful pale pink flowers and long edible fruits which give it the name of Banana Fruited Passion Flower. *P. amethystina,* a glorious blue-purple, *P. antioquiensis,* shocking pink, *P. caeruleo-racemosa* a hybrid with very freely produced purple flowers and another hybrid *P. × allardii* of subtle pinks and purples are all recommended for the warm house. *P. coccinea* is spectacular for the tropical house with its bright red flowers. *P. racemosa* is also tropical but is smaller growing and bears fewer, though interesting, dark reddish-purple flowers.

Plants are easily raised from seed or by cuttings in May or June. After flowering plants can be pruned hard, cutting back the flowered shoots to within a bud or two of older wood. It is inadvisable to cut into very old wood without leaving a younger spur as they may fail to grow back. Be ever vigilant against red spider mite which love to attack them and, to a lesser extent, mealy bug.

Pavonia   W/T   family *Malvaceae*

Pavonia multiflora from Brazil is a most attractive plant with bright red and purple flowers. It does better under tropical conditions where it will flower for a longer period at the end of the summer. Propagation is by seed which is freely produced or by cuttings which can be taken when the plant is cut back. Unpruned, specimens will become very tall and lose lower leaves so it pays to prune hard when this stage is reached.

Pelargonium   C/W   family *Geraniaceae*   South Africa and St Helena

Originally, because their seed pods all looked like cranes' bills, a whole group of plants were lumped together in Geraniaceae and called Geraniums. However, Linnaeus later decided that there were important differences between the hardy border *Geranium* and what we should now call *Pelargonium*. Unfortunately, the old name of Geranium has stuck leading to some confusion.

Only *Pelargonium cotyledonis,* the Old Man Geranium, comes from St Helena; all the other species are from South Africa. When the tea clippers called in at the Cape the captains, if they had time, would pick up a few species and deliver them back to various parts of Europe into the hands of the head gardeners of the big estate gardens. Thus, 21 different species chosen at random by non horticulturalists and hybridised by the gardeners gave rise to all the Pelargoniums we have today. Not only did different varieties arise by crossing plants to get seed but by plants producing sports, or parts of the plant which are different from the rest, which can be removed and propagated to give a new variety. The first type of Pelargonium to arise as a result of hybridising was the Regal followed by the Uniques and Shrubland Pets which were originally used for bedding out. Finally the modern Zonal Pelargoniums were bred which have proved to be the toughest and whose flowers last the longest. All the Pelargoniums make excellent greenhouse plants. The Zonals make good bedding plants but to my way of thinking real satisfaction lies in growing a named collection of species and varieties under glass where they will bloom magnificently, unaffected by the ravages of typical British summers. There are also those which flower better in winter.

Cultivation depends to an extent on which type of Pelargonium you are dealing with. Regals are propagated by cuttings towards the end of summer and grown on warm throughout the winter to flower in May and June. These plants should have the tips pinched out throughout their growth to give a good bushy shape to the plant and lots of flower heads. Zonal Pelargoniums like to be kept very much on the dry side and prefer a loam-based compost. Overwatering leads to the leaves turning yellow or sometimes bright red and dropping off. If plants are being overwintered in frost free temperatures they can be cut right back to remove all the leaves and kept almost completely dry

141

throughout winter. Cuttings that might have been taken in autumn need a bit more warmth and watering to keep them going through winter. I pinch the tips out of cuttings at 5–8 cm (2–3 in) tall. Keep the species and scented leaved types growing all year round, being much more careful about the watering in winter. Occasionally, the taller ones will need to be cut back; best done in spring. Some of the species have tuberous roots or very succulent stems. These will become dormant during winter and should not be watered until they grow again in spring. Apart from Regals, cuttings should not be given humidity in which to root, preferring to stand on the open staging in pots of peat and grit allowed to become dry between waterings. Great care must be taken with cuttings especially of Zonals in autumn as they are prone to a fungal disease known as black leg. Treatment with the appropiate fungicide as a precaution may be necessary. The other main problem is rust which affects the Zonals. Rust spores overwinter on leaves; if your plants have been badly infected this is why you should cut plants back to remove all the leaves in autumn which should then be burned. The plants will break into growth the following spring.

My personal favourites are the species which can be obtained either as plants or seed sown in spring at a temperature of 13°C (55°F). *P. quinquelobatum* has small curiously coloured flowers which manage to be almost but neither grey, blue nor green. A large clay pot of *P. triste,* which is tuberous, makes a fine sight with its carroty foliage and pale yellow flowers.

Pellionia   S   family *Urticaceae*

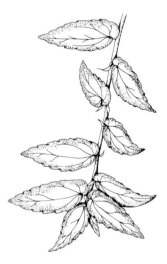

Pellionia daveauana

Pellionia daveauana from Burma, Vietnam and Malaysia is a trailing foliage plant that needs tropical conditions to do well. I like to plant six or seven rooted cuttings into a large pan of peat-based compost and use this as an edging plant for displays of taller plants. Cuttings are extremely easy to root at virtually any time of the year. Alternatively, their attractive dark and apple green leaves will look lovely tumbling over the sides of a hanging basket.

Pentas   W   family *Rubiaceae*   Africa and Madagascar

Pentas lanceolata makes a pretty plant for a warm house and is best planted out where it will grow into a small shrub bearing its pink starry flowers most during autumn. Cuttings root easily or seed can be sown in spring at 18–21°C (65–70°F). Pinching out the tips of shoots to make the plants bushier will give better specimens with more flower heads. I have never found that pruning these plants is satisfactory as they seem to grow back in a weak straggly fashion. When old plants have become scrappy it is best to have anticipated this and have a new batch raised. Seed of mixed dwarf hybrids is now available which grows into small 45-cm (18-in) high plants ideal for pots. Flower colours are from white through different pinks to red.

Peperomia   W/T   family *Piperaceae*

The nice things about these plants is that as they are mostly small a good collection can be grown without taking up too much space. The most important thing to remember is that they cannot stand being overwatered and will quickly rot at the roots and die. In the wild they would grow in shallow soil perhaps around the trunks and roots of trees. A well-drained peat-based compost will suit them best. They will grow much faster in tropical conditions but will grow adequately in a warm house. The common name of Pepper Elder will do for them all but probably the most commonly grown is *Peperomia caperata* with its crinkly leaves and long creamy flower spikes held well above the leaves. This can be propagated by leaf cuttings (see page 25) or cuttings of short stems. The variegated form cannot be grown from leaf cuttings as they will always revert to green. *P. obtusifolia* 'Variegeta' has quite hectic variegation of greens, yellow and cream and often goes wrongly under the name of *P. magnoliafolia* 'Variegata' which has much longer leaves. *P. sandersii (P. argyreia)* from Brazil has heart-shaped leaves with attractive bands of green and silver which have given it the name Watermelon Peperomia. The one with the most attractive flowers is *P. resediflora* from Colombia. *P. incana* from Brazil is unusual in having long shoots with leaves covered in white hairs giving it a silvery appearance. There are many others, all sufficiently different from each other to make a very attractive group.

143

Peristrophe   W   family *Acanthaceae*

Peristrophe angustifolia from Java is a trailing plant which is good for baskets. Usually *P. a.* 'Aurea Variegata' is grown which has a pale yellow mark down the middle of the leaf. The bright pink flowers are freely produced. Like many others in the same family they require a lot of work to keep them looking good and fresh; as they grow quickly they can become very tatty if not constantly cut back and eventually replaced by new material raised from the very easy-to-root cuttings. *P. speciosa* is a bright reliable plant for winter flowering colour in a warm house. It adds to the Christmas atmosphere created by Poinsettias and *Cyclamen*. Bright pinky-purple flowers nearly 5 cm (2 in) long appear on bushy plants 90 cm (3 ft) high. After flowering the plants should be pruned hard back and rested slightly before being encouraged to grow in spring. Cuttings should be taken in April and grown on well, pinching out the growing points two or three times up until July to produce good sized plants for next year's flowers.

Petrea   W/T   family *Verbenaceae*

Petrea volubilis is the Purple Wreath from Mexico, Central America and the West Indies. It is a very attractive and unusual climber in that it has sprays of bright blue flowers which in Britain in warm conditions are produced from late spring. In the wild they are in flower almost continuously with two short rest periods in winter and late summer. I have to admit to never seeing this plant for sale in Britain, but I should imagine they are more available in the USA. Plants are better in tropical conditions but will still give a good display of flowers in cooler temperatures. If possible, plant them out and give them a support up which to climb. Long shoots can be cut back by a good two-thirds once flowering is over but they should then be left as flowers are formed on the previous year's growth. It also pays to give plants a brief rest after flowering; reducing the water and stopping the feed. After a month of this they can be grown on well again.

Phaseolus   T   family *Leguminosae*

Phaseolus caracalla is the Snail Plant from tropical America. At Wisley I discovered one of these that had sat in its pot in a corner for years, rather anonymously as it had lost its label, doing nothing at all; every so often somebody would come by with some secateurs and cut what straggly growth it had made back. When a climber had to be replaced I planted the then unknown plant into a shallow border of peat-based compost and within 18 months it had grown enormous and produced curious, highly scented snail-shaped pinkish-white flowers. After flowering it is best to prune the plant back to its somewhat swollen rootstock, leaving a few nodes on newish growth behind. After a rest during the winter when it should be kept on the dry side it will sprout afresh in spring; watch out for red spider mite. I am delighted to see that seed is obtainable. Apparently Australians used to grow this plant a lot outside in the hotter parts of their country to cover their outside lavatories. With the disappearance of these structures in modern times the plant has almost been lost to cultivation in that country.

Philodendron   T   family *Araceae*   Tropical America

Although able to struggle along under warm conditions these foliage plants are much better in a stove house. Some of them are huge in which case probably only one stately specimen would be enough for most greenhouses. Smaller ones include *Philodendron scandens* the popular Sweet Heart Plant so called because of its heart-shaped leaves. This will either climb or grow in a hanging basket. *P. erubescens* with its shiny dark green leaves with copper undersides remains a reasonable size. *P. verrucosum* with its paler mossy green leaves and bristly green leaf stalks is also of moderate size. *P.* 'Burgundy', which has reddish young leaves and pinky-purple stems and undersides, will be a large climber very quickly. *P. bipinnatifidum* does not climb at first but becomes a huge plant with massive indented leaves. *P. selloum* is very similar but its leaves have far fewer, less extreme incisions. *P. wendlandii* does not climb but does form a thick stalk; it too will become a very grand plant. Seed is available, especially of *P. scandens, P. selloum* and *P. bipinnatifidum*. Contrary to what you might think large specimens 60–90 cm (2–3ft) tall can be had within two or three years. Only just cover seed and germinate at 24–26°C (75–80°F). Cuttings are easy to take of types which grow reasonable stems. Cut stem sections with two leaves, cutting above the top one and below the bottom one which should then be cut off. Root at 24–26°C (75–80°F).

Pilea   W   family *Urticaceae*

A useful group of small plants. *Pilea cadierei* commonly known as the Aluminium Plant is the best known. It has pretty foliage, the dark green leaves are patterned with raised silver patches. *P. mollis* 'Moon Valley' is also well known for its moss green and copper coloured leaves. *P. spruceana* 'Norfolk' is different again; leaves being striped silver and bronze. All are very easy to grow

145

providing the temperature is constantly warm and they are not overwatered. *P. microphylla* is widely grown throughout parks departments and botanic gardens but for some reason is not usually for sale. The leaves are tiny hence the name, although it is sometimes called *P. muscosa*. It is supposed to be the Artillery Plant because of the minute flowers exploding their cloud of pollen over a long distance. Although I have handled them a lot I have never witnessed this strange event. I have, however, seen its close relative *Pellionia daveauana* perform in a similar way and it was fairly spectacular. Cuttings of these plants may be taken at virtually any time of the year as they are very easy to root.

Piper   T   family *Piperaceae*   Tropical America

The only species widely grown is *Piper ornatum* from Celebes which needs tropical conditions and either a climbing frame or space to trail down. The leaves are green with a speckling of pink and silver. The backs of the leaves are bright maroon especially when the light shines through them. I would grow them in a light peat-based soil as their root system is never very well developed. When they are established liquid feed regularly. Cuttings are by sections of stem each with two nodes. Cut above the top one, below the bottom one and then cut the bottom leaf off. Rooting will take place quickest at 24°C (75°F).

Pittosporum   FF/C   family *Pittosporaceae*

Although most of these can be grown outside albeit in a sheltered place *Pittosporum tobira* from China and Japan is only half hardy and a good candidate for the greenhouse. Unlike the daintily leafed species used for flower arrangements this one has comparatively large oval leaves. It will remain a shrub of 1.2 m (4 ft) if planted in a pot but may become a little taller if planted in the border. It has cream coloured orange blossom-scented flowers during summer. The variegated form is particularly attractive. Cuttings preferably of semi ripe wood with a heel are best taken in late summer. Alternatively, seed is available which surprisingly enough germinates better if dipped into boiling water for a few seconds. A temperature of 13°C (55°F) is best for germination.

Plectranthus   W   family *Labiatae*

I have my reservations whether anybody with limited greenhouse space would want to sacrifice valuable room to grow these. *Plectranthus coleoides* 'Marginatus' from India will grow upright to about 30 cm (1 ft) before

146

bending over and trailing. Its leaves have a strange, not unpleasant smell when crushed. It will eventually bear rather insignificant white flowers. *P. oertendahlii* from South Africa is a rather chaotic plant with rounded leaves with white veins, red undersides and white flowers. The fleshy stems are pink. *P. ciliatus* is perhaps a bit more inspiring as it has mauve-blue flowers in late summer.

Plumbago   C/T   family *Plumbaginaceae*

Plumbago rosea

Plumbago capensis from South Africa makes a lovely climbing plant for the cool house. Ideally they should be planted out but will still flower as small plants in pots. The beautiful clear blue flowers are freely produced in late summer, almost covering the whole plant. There is also *P. c.* 'Alba' the white form which is just as enthusiastic a flowerer. However, be careful to plant it where its white flowers will stand out; I had one once that flowered against the sky which was invariably white and consequently the flowers never showed up. After flowering the plants should be cut back hard to within a few nodes of older wood. Do not, however, make the mistake of pruning old plants too hard or they will do little more than send out a few wispy shoots from the old wood. Cuttings 8–10 cm (3–4 in) long should root with no trouble at 21°C (70°F) and plants will flower in their second year from spring sown seed placed in 21–24°C (70–75°F). There is a tropical species cultivated; *P. rosea* from the

147